# Manhattan Review

## Test Prep & Admissions Consulting

# Turbocharge Your SAT:
# Passport to Advanced Math Guide

part of the 2nd Edition Series

April 20th, 2016

☐ *Designed as per the Revised SAT*

☐ *Text-cum-graphic explanations of concepts*

☐ *100 SAT-like practice questions*

☐ *Inclusion of the topics:*

  ○ *Quadratic equations*

  ○ *Quadratic functions and their graphs*

  ○ *Polynomial expressions*

  ○ *Factoring polynomial*

  ○ *Advanced equations*

  ○ *Application of functions*

☐ *Many questions with Alternate approaches*

☐ *Great collection of questions on 'Higher order Thinking'*

☐ *Each question tagged with 'With calculator' or 'Without calculator'*

# www.manhattanreview.com

# Copyright and Terms of Use

## Copyright and Trademark

All materials herein (including names, terms, trademarks, designs, images, and graphics) are the property of Manhattan Review, except where otherwise noted. Except as permitted herein, no such material may be copied, reproduced, displayed or transmitted or otherwise used without the prior written permission of Manhattan Review. You are permitted to use material herein for your personal, non-commercial use, provided that you do not combine such material into a combination, collection, or compilation of material. If you have any questions regarding the use of the material, please contact Manhattan Review at info@manhattanreview.com.

This material may make reference to countries and persons. The use of such references is for hypothetical and demonstrative purposes only.

## Terms of Use

By using this material, you acknowledge and agree to the terms of use contained herein.

## No Warranties

This material is provided without warranty, either express or implied, including the implied warranties of merchantability, of fitness for a particular purpose and noninfringement. Manhattan Review does not warrant or make any representations regarding the use, accuracy or results of the use of this material. This material may make reference to other source materials. Manhattan Review is not responsible in any respect for the content of such other source materials, and disclaims all warranties and liabilities with respect to the other source materials.

## Limitation on Liability

Manhattan Review shall not be responsible under any circumstances for any direct, indirect, special, punitive, or consequential damages ("Damages") that may arise from the use of this material. In addition, Manhattan Review does not guarantee the accuracy or completeness of its course materials, which are provided "as is" with no warranty, express or implied. Manhattan Review assumes no liability for any Damages from errors or omissions in the material, whether arising in contract, tort or otherwise.

10-Digit International Standard Book Number: (ISBN: 1-62926-093-2)
13-Digit International Standard Book Number: (ISBN: 978-1-62926-093-8)

Last updated on April 20th, 2016.

Manhattan Review, 275 Madison Avenue, Suite 1429, New York, NY 10016.
Phone: +1 (212) 316-2000. E-Mail: info@manhattanreview.com. Web: www.manhattanreview.com

## About the Turbocharge your SAT Series

The Turbocharge Your SAT Series was created to provide students with comprehensive and highly effective SAT preparation for maximum SAT performance. Thousands of students around the world have received substantial score improvements by using Manhattan Review's SAT prep books. Now in its updated 2nd edition for the new SAT in 2016, the full series of 12 guides is designed to provide SAT students with rigorous, thorough, and accessible SAT instruction for top SAT scores. Manhattan Review's SAT prep books precisely target each testing area and deconstruct the different test sections in a manner that is both student-centered and results-driven, teaching test-takers everything they need to know in order to significantly boost their scores. Covering all of the necessary material in mathematics and verbal skills from the most basic through the most advanced levels, the Turbocharge Your SAT Series is the top study resource for all stages of SAT preparation. Students who work through the complete series develop all of the skills, knowledge, and strategies needed for their best possible SAT scores.

- ☐ **SAT Math Essentials (ISBN: 978-1-62926-090-7)**
- ☐ **SAT Heart of Algebra Guide (ISBN: 978-1-62926-091-4)**
- ☐ **SAT Problem Solving & Data Analysis Guide (ISBN: 978-1-62926-092-1)**
- ☑ **SAT Passport to Advanced Math Guide (ISBN: 978-1-62926-093-8)**
- ☐ **SAT Advanced Topics in Math Guide (ISBN: 978-1-62926-095-2)**
- ☐ **SAT Practice Tests (ISBN: 978-1-62926-096-9)**
- ☐ **SAT Quantitative Question Bank (ISBN: 978-1-62926-097-6)**
- ☐ **SAT Critical Reading Guide (ISBN: 978-1-62926-098-3)**
- ☐ **SAT Writing & Language Test Guide (ISBN: 978-1-62926-099-0)**
- ☐ **SAT Essay Guide (ISBN: 978-1-62926-100-3)**
- ☐ **SAT Vocabulary Builder (ISBN: 978-1-62926-101-0)**

Passport to Advanced Math Guide

## About the Company

Manhattan Review's origin can be traced directly back to an Ivy League MBA classroom in 1999. While teaching advanced quantitative subjects to MBAs at Columbia Business School in New York City, Professor Dr. Joern Meissner developed a reputation for explaining complicated concepts in an understandable way. Prof. Meissner's students challenged him to assist their friends, who were frustrated with conventional test preparation options. In response, Prof. Meissner created original lectures that focused on presenting standardized test content in a simplified and intelligible manner, a method vastly different from the voluminous memorization and so-called tricks commonly offered by others. The new methodology immediately proved highly popular with students, inspiring the birth of Manhattan Review.

Since its founding, Manhattan Review has grown into a multi-national educational services firm, focusing on preparation for the major undergraduate and graduate admissions tests, college admissions consulting, and application advisory services, with thousands of highly satisfied students all over the world. Our SAT instruction is continuously expanded and updated by the Manhattan Review team, an enthusiastic group of master SAT professionals and senior academics. Our team ensures that Manhattan Review offers the most time-efficient and cost-effective preparation available for the SAT. Please visit www.ManhattanReview.com for further details.

## About the Founder

Professor Dr. Joern Meissner has more than 25 years of teaching experience at the graduate and undergraduate levels. He is the founder of Manhattan Review, a worldwide leader in test prep services, and he created the original lectures for its first test preparation classes. Prof. Meissner is a graduate of Columbia Business School in New York City, where he received a PhD in Management Science. He has since served on the faculties of prestigious business schools in the United Kingdom and Germany. He is a recognized authority in the areas of supply chain management, logistics, and pricing strategy. Prof. Meissner thoroughly enjoys his research, but he believes that grasping an idea is only half of the fun. Conveying knowledge to others is even more fulfilling. This philosophy was crucial to the establishment of Manhattan Review, and remains its most cherished principle.

www.manhattanreview.com

© 1999–2016 Manhattan Review

# International Phone Numbers and Official Manhattan Review Websites

| | | |
|---|---|---|
| Manhattan Headquarters | +1-212-316-2000 | www.manhattanreview.com |
| USA & Canada | +1-800-246-4600 | www.manhattanreview.com |
| Argentina | +1-212-316-2000 | www.review.com.ar |
| Australia | +61-3-9001-6618 | www.manhattanreview.com |
| Austria | +43-720-115-549 | www.review.at |
| Belgium | +32-2-808-5163 | www.manhattanreview.be |
| Brazil | +1-212-316-2000 | www.manhattanreview.com.br |
| Chile | +1-212-316-2000 | www.manhattanreview.cl |
| China | +86-20-2910-1913 | www.manhattanreview.cn |
| Czech Republic | +1-212-316-2000 | www.review.cz |
| France | +33-1-8488-4204 | www.review.fr |
| Germany | +49-89-3803-8856 | www.review.de |
| Greece | +1-212-316-2000 | www.review.com.gr |
| Hong Kong | +852-5808-2704 | www.review.hk |
| Hungary | +1-212-316-2000 | www.review.co.hu |
| India | +1-212-316-2000 | www.review.in |
| Indonesia | +1-212-316-2000 | www.manhattanreview.id |
| Ireland | +1-212-316-2000 | www.gmat.ie |
| Italy | +39-06-9338-7617 | www.manhattanreview.it |
| Japan | +81-3-4589-5125 | www.manhattanreview.jp |
| Malaysia | +1-212-316-2000 | www.review.my |
| Netherlands | +31-20-808-4399 | www.manhattanreview.nl |
| New Zealand | +1-212-316-2000 | www.review.co.nz |
| Philippines | +1-212-316-2000 | www.review.ph |
| Poland | +1-212-316-2000 | www.review.pl |
| Portugal | +1-212-316-2000 | www.review.pt |
| Qatar | +1-212-316-2000 | www.review.qa |
| Russia | +1-212-316-2000 | www.manhattanreview.ru |
| Singapore | +65-3158-2571 | www.gmat.sg |
| South Africa | +1-212-316-2000 | www.manhattanreview.co.za |
| South Korea | +1-212-316-2000 | www.manhattanreview.kr |
| Sweden | +1-212-316-2000 | www.gmat.se |
| Spain | +34-911-876-504 | www.review.es |
| Switzerland | +41-435-080-991 | www.review.ch |
| Taiwan | +1-212-316-2000 | www.gmat.tw |
| Thailand | +66-6-0003-5529 | www.manhattanreview.com |
| Turkey | +1-212-316-2000 | www.review.com.tr |
| United Arab Emirates | +1-212-316-2000 | www.manhattanreview.ae |
| United Kingdom | +44-20-7060-9800 | www.manhattanreview.co.uk |
| Rest of World | +1-212-316-2000 | www.manhattanreview.com |

# Contents

# Chapter 1

# Welcome

Dear Students,

Here at Manhattan Review, we constantly strive to provide you the best educational content for standardized test preparation. We make a tremendous effort to keep making things better and better for you. This is especially important with respect to an examination such as the SAT. As you know that from Spring'16, SAT goes for a major change. The revised SAT is challenging now.

The revised SAT will focus more on **Algebra** and **Data Analysis**. Manhattan Review's SAT-Passport to Advanced Math Guide has a collection of 100 questions Including: **Quadratic equations, Quadratic functions and their graphs, Polynomial expressions, Factoring polynomial, Advanced equations, Application of functions**, and **Higher Order Thinking**. There are ample questions related to the concept of **Higher Order Thinking**. As you know that there would be a 'No-Calculator' math section, so we have tagged each of the 100 questions with either 'With calculator' or 'Without calculator'.

In a nut shell, Manhattan Review's SAT-Passport to Advanced Math Guide is holistic and comprehensive for the practice; it is created so because we listen to what students need. Should you have any query, please feel free to write to us at info@manhattanreview.com.

Happy Learning!

Professor Dr. Joern Meissner
& The Manhattan Review Team

# Chapter 2

# Introduction to The Revised SAT

The SAT has changed and the Revised SAT will take effect in the Spring of 2016. The revised SAT will comprise two major sections: one, Evidence-based Reading & Writing and two, Math. The essay, which now is optional is excluded from being a compulsory part of SAT Writing section. Evidence-based Reading & Writing has two sections: one, Reading (only Reading, no Critical word prefixed to it, but that does not mean that the new Reading Test will not test critical aspects of reading) and two, Writing & Language Test. This section has gone for a major change in its format. Questions testing your skills at writing, grammar, & language aspects will be taken up from a passage. With both Reading & Writing & Language sections being passage-based, they may also include info-graphics within the passages, and there would be one or two questions based on a graph or a chart. You may have a flavor of some math in the Reading passages & the Writing passages.

While the format of the Math test remains unchanged, there are new additions in Math section. It will focus more on Algebra and Data Analysis. You will see more questions on real-life situational charts and graphs in the test. There is an addition of two new topics: Trigonometry & Complex Numbers. There would be one or two questions testing your higher order thinking. Those questions may be in a set of two questions and would have a lengthy narration. Another special category of questions would be one in which you would be asked to interpret a situation described mathematically in word; there would be four options, each being at least two lines, and only one of the options is correct. Another change to the math section is that there would be a section of No-Calculator.

Two noticeable changes in the Revised SAT are: one, there is no negative marking and two, there would be only four options in MCQs.

## 2.1   The Old SAT vs. The Revised SAT

|  | Old SAT | Revised SAT |
|---|---|---|
| Sections | • Math<br><br>• Critical Reading<br><br>• Writing (incl. Essay) | • Math<br><br>• Evidence-based Reading & Writing<br>  ○ Reading<br>  ○ Writing & Language Test<br><br>• Essay (optional; exclusive of Writing & Language test) |
| Content | • Reasoning Skills<br><br>• Contextual vocabulary<br><br>• Applied mathematical problems | • Reasoning Skills & knowledge of real-world situations<br><br>• Evidence-based Reading, Writing, & Math problems<br><br>• Introduction of graphs & charts in passages, thereby testing associated questions (even calculation-based questions)<br><br>• Contextual vocabulary in broader contexts<br><br>• Introduction of Trigonometry & Complex Numbers in math<br><br>• Higher Order thinking questions in math |
| Question types | • Multiple Choice Questions (MCQ)<br><br>• Student-produced response Questions (Grid-In) in math | • Multiple Choice Questions (MCQ)<br><br>• Student-produced response Questions (Grid-In) in math |
| Number of options for MCQs | 5 ( A through E) | 4 (A through D) |
| Negative marking | $-\frac{1}{4}$ for wrong answer | No negative marking |

| Scoring | • Total score: 600–2400; incl. scores from Critical Reading, Writing, & Math (each score from 200–800)<br><br>• Writing score includes Essay score | • Total score: 400–1600; incl. scores from Evidence-based Reading and Writing, & Math (each scored from 200–800)<br><br>• Essays are scored separately (1–4)<br><br>• Sub-scores & Cross-scores (contribution from selected areas) |
|---|---|---|
| Timing | • 3 hours 45 minutes | • 3 hours (excluding essay)<br><br>• 3 hours 50 minutes (including essay) |
| Calculator access | Throughout the math section | There would be a No-Calculator section in the math section |

## 2.2 Revised SAT Math content

| Content | Topics | Number of questions | |
|---|---|---|---|
| | | Calculator | No-Calculator |
| Heart of Algebra | Fundamental concepts used in Algebra; arranging formulae, linear equations, inequalities, etc. | 11 | 8 |
| Problem Solving & Data Analysis | Understanding qualitative & quantitative data, analyzing relationship, incl. graphical; Ratio & Proportion, Percents, and units of measurements | 17 | None (All questions with calculator acess) |
| Passport to Advanced Math | Advanced concepts in Algebra, incl. quadratic & higher order equations, polynomials | 7 | 9 |
| Advanced topics in Math | Geometry (2D, area, volume; & 3D), Trigonometry, Complex numbers | 3 | 3 |
| | **Total number of questions (58) Total time (80 minutes)** | **38 (55 minutes)** | **20 (25 minutes)** |

# Chapter 3

# Concepts

## 3.1   Quadratic Equations

An equation is said to be quadratic when the variable contains the highest exponent of '2', thus $ax^2 + bx + c$ is a quadratic expression in one variable i.e. of $x$.

**Solving a Quadratic Equation by Factorization:**

A quadratic equation can be solved quickly if it can be written in the form of a product of two linear expressions.

Let us take an example:

$2x^2 - 7x + 6 = 0$

The given equation can be written as:

$2x^2 - 4x - 3x + 6 = 0$

While dividing the middle term in two parts, it should be seen that the product of the two terms equals the product of the first and last terms of the quadratic.

Thus, here we have: $(-4x) \times (-3x) = (2x^2) \times (6) = 12x^2$

$=> 2x(x - 2) - 3(x - 2) = 0$

$=> (2x - 3)(x - 2) = 0$

Here, $2x - 3$ and $x - 2$ are the two linear expressions. Since their product is 0, at least one of them must be 0.

This results in two separate linear equations:

$2x - 3 = 0$

OR

$x - 2 = 0$

$=> x = \dfrac{3}{2}$  OR  $x = 2$

Thus, each quadratic equation can be written in the form $(x - p)(x - q) = 0$, where $p$ and $q$ are the roots of the quadratic equation.

**Roots of a Quadratic Equation:**

After suitable reduction, every quadratic equation can be written in the form:

$ax^2 + bx + c = 0$

The solution or the roots of the above equation is given by:

$$p = \frac{-b + \sqrt{b^2 - 4ac}}{2a} \text{ and } q = \frac{-b - \sqrt{b^2 - 4ac}}{2a}; \text{ where } p \text{ and } q \text{ are the roots}$$

Let us see how:

$$ax^2 + bx + c = 0$$

Dividing throughout by $a$:

$$x^2 + \frac{b}{a}x + \frac{c}{a} = 0$$

Let us combine the first two terms of the above equation to form a perfect square:

$$=> x^2 + 2x\left(\frac{b}{2a}\right) + \left(\frac{b}{2a}\right)^2 - \left(\frac{b}{2a}\right)^2 + \frac{c}{a} = 0$$

$$=> \left(x + \frac{b}{2a}\right)^2 = \left(\frac{b}{2a}\right)^2 - \frac{c}{a} = \frac{b^2 - 4ac}{4a^2}$$

Taking square roots on both sides:

$$=> x + \frac{b}{2a} = \pm\sqrt{\frac{b^2 - 4ac}{4a^2}} = \pm\frac{\sqrt{b^2 - 4ac}}{2a}$$

$$=> x = -\frac{b}{2a} \pm \frac{\sqrt{b^2 - 4ac}}{2a}$$

$$=> x = \frac{-b \pm \sqrt{b^2 - 4ac}}{2a}$$

Let us find the roots of the previous equation $2x^2 - 7x + 6 = 0$ using the above formula:

We have: $a = 2$, $b = -7$, $c = 6$

Thus, the roots are:

$$\frac{-b \pm \sqrt{b^2 - 4ac}}{2a} = \frac{-(-7) \pm \sqrt{(-7)^2 - 4(2)(6)}}{2(2)} = \frac{7 \pm 1}{4} = \frac{7-1}{4} \text{ OR } \frac{7+1}{4} = \frac{3}{2} \text{ OR } 2$$

**Discriminant:**

The value given by $D(\triangle) = b^2 - 4ac$, i.e. the quantity under the square root, is called the discriminant and depending upon its value we can determine the nature of the roots of the quadratic equations:

- If $D \geq 0$: The roots are real
- If $D = 0$: The roots are real and equal
- If $D > 0$: The roots are real and unequal
- If $D < 0$: The roots are imaginary or complex
- If D is a perfect square: The roots are real and rational
- If D is not a perfect square: The roots are real and irrational (one root is conjugate of the other, i.e. the roots are of the form $a \pm \sqrt{b}$)

Let us take some example

- In the equation $x^2 + 2x + 1 = 0$, $D = b^2 - 4ac = 2^2 - 4.(1).(1) = 0$
  => The roots are real and equal.

- In the equation $x^2 + 2x + 2 = 0$, $D = b^2 - 4ac = 2^2 - 4.(1).(2) = -4 < 0$
  => The roots are complex.

**Sum and Product of the roots:**

If the roots of the quadratic equation $ax^2 + bx + c = 0$ are $p$ and $q$, we have:

$$ax^2 + bx + c \equiv a(x - p)(x - q)$$

$$=> ax^2 + bx + c \equiv a(x^2 - x(p + q) + pq)$$

$$=> ax^2 + bx + c \equiv ax^2 - a(p + q)x + apq$$

Comparing the coefficient of $x$ and the constant term, we have:

$$b = -a(p + q) \text{ and } c = apq$$

$$=> p + q = -\frac{b}{a} \text{ and } pq = \frac{c}{a}$$

**Expressing a quadratic equation in terms of its roots:**

Suppose we have to form the equation whose roots are $p$ and $q$.

Thus, we have: $(x - p) = 0$ and $(x - q) = 0$

$$=> (x - p)(x - q) = 0$$

$$=> x^2 - x(p + q) + pq = 0$$

$$=> \mathbf{x^2 - (\text{Sum of roots})\, x + (\text{Product of roots}) = 0}$$

Let us take an example:

The equation having roots $-2$ and $5$ is:

$$x^2 - (-2 + 5)x + (-2)(5) = 0$$

$$=> x^2 - 3x - 10 = 0$$

**Expressing a quadratic equation in terms of its vertex:**

Let the equation be

$$y = ax^2 + bx + c$$

$$= a\left\{x^2 + \left(\frac{b}{a}\right)x + \frac{c}{a}\right\}$$

$$= a\left\{\left(x + \frac{b}{2a}\right)^2 - \left(\frac{b}{2a}\right)^2 + \frac{c}{a}\right\}$$

$$= a\left(x + \frac{b}{2a}\right)^2 - \frac{(b^2 - 4ac)}{4a}$$

$$= a(x - h)^2 - k; \text{ here, } h = -\frac{b}{2a} \text{ and } k = \frac{(b^2 - 4ac)}{4a}$$

The coordinates of the vertex is given by $(h, k)$.

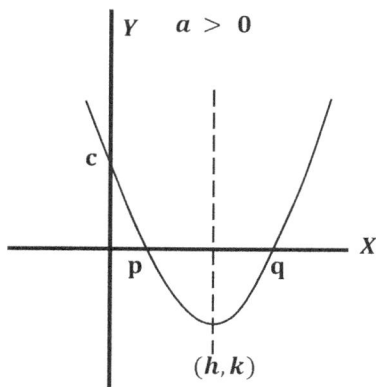

**The line of
symmetry: $x = h$**

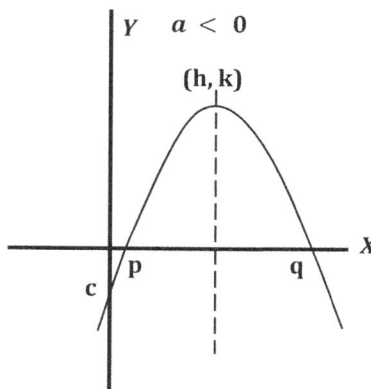

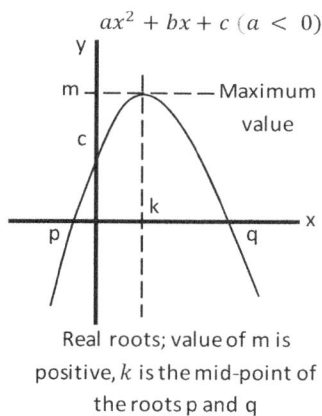

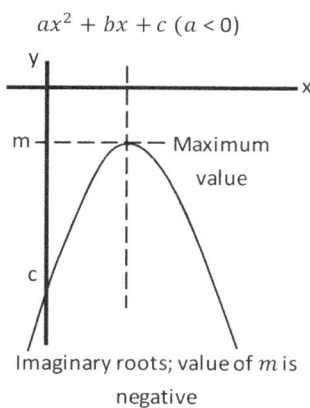

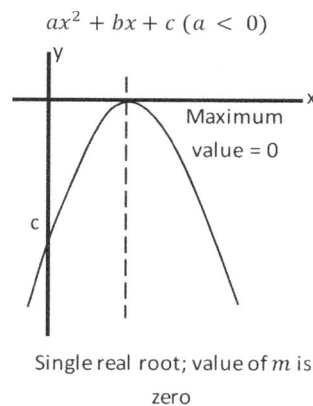

**The line of
symmetry: $x = h$**

Real roots; value of m is
positive, $k$ is the mid-point of
the roots p and q

Imaginary roots; value of $m$ is
negative

Single real root; value of $m$ is
zero

**Additional solved problems:**

(1) A man can swim in still water (without any current) at a rate of 4 miles per hour. He undertakes to swim from point A to point B and back, in a river which has a current of its own. If the distance between the points A and B is 15 miles, and the total time he takes for the trip is 8 hours, what is the rate of flow of the river current in miles per hour?

Note: While swimming against the river, the man's normal swimming rate would be reduced by the amount of the rate of the current, similarly, while going along with the flow of the river, his speed would be increased by the rate of the current.

Explanation:

Let the rate of the river current be $r$ miles per hour.

Since the man makes a round trip, one way he would be swimming against the river, while the other way, he would be swimming with the river.

Thus, while swimming against the river, the rate of the man = $(4 - r)$ miles per hour

Thus, time taken to cover 15 miles = $\left(\dfrac{15}{4-r}\right)$ hours.

While swimming with the river, the rate of the man = $(4 + r)$ miles per hour

Thus, time taken to cover 15 miles = $\left(\dfrac{15}{4+r}\right)$ hours.

Since the total time is 8 hours, we have:

$$\dfrac{15}{4-r} + \dfrac{15}{4+r} = 8$$

$$=> 15(4 + r + 4 - r) = 8(4^2 - r^2)$$

$$=> 8r^2 = 8 \times 4^2 - 15 \times 8 = 128 - 120$$

$$=> 8r^2 = 8 => r^2 = 1$$

$$=> r = 1$$

(2) A man buys a number of pieces of chocolates for $24. If the price of a piece of chocolate increases by $2, he can buy 1 piece of chocolate less for the same amount. What is the price of 1 piece of chocolate?

Explanation:

Let the price of a piece of chocolate be $x$.

Thus, the number of chocolate pieces the man can buy for \$24 = $\left(\dfrac{24}{x}\right)$

New price of a piece of chocolate = \$ $(x + 2)$.

Thus, the number of chocolate pieces the man can now buy for \$24 = $\left(\dfrac{24}{x+2}\right)$

Since the number of pieces of chocolate is 1 less than the previous occassion, we have:

$$\frac{24}{x+2} = \frac{24}{x} - 1$$

$$=> \frac{24}{x} - \frac{24}{x+2} = 1$$

$$=> \frac{24(x+2-x)}{x(x+2)} = 1$$

$$=> x(x+2) = 48$$

Since $48 = 6 \times 8$, we have:

$$x = 6$$

Alternately, we can solve the quadratic:

$$x(x+2) = 48 => x^2 + 2x - 48 = 0$$

$$=> (x+8)(x-6) = 0$$

$$=> x = 6$$

(3) The total cost, in dollars, of manufacturing $n$ items of a product is given by $(2n^2 + 30)$. The selling price of each item is fixed at \$36. What is the number of items that must be sold so as to have maximum profit?

Explanation:

Total cost of manufacturing $n$ items = \$ $(2n^2 + 30)$.

Selling price of each item = \$36.

Thus, total selling price of $n$ items = \$ $(36n)$.

Thus, profit earned = Selling price − Cost price

$$= 36n - (2n^2 + 30)$$

$$= -2\left(n^2 - 18n + 15\right)$$

$$= -2\left(n^2 - 18n + 81 - 66\right)$$

$$= -2(n - 9)^2 + 132$$

The profit would be maximized if the negative square term, i.e. $-2(n-9)^2$ becomes '0', which happens when $n = 9$.

The corresponding maximum value of the profit is \$132.

## 3.2 Inequalities

(1) **Number line based inequalities**: There are four important regions on a number line, as shown below:

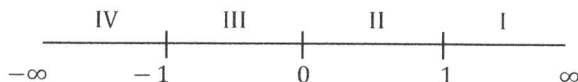

Some properties of the above four regions:

○ **Region I**: A number $x$ in the region satisfies $1 < x < \infty$

Higher the exponent of $x$, higher is the value of the term and vice versa.
Thus, we have:
$x < x^2 < x^3 \ldots$ For example: $2 < 2^2 < 2^3$
$x > \sqrt{x} > \sqrt[3]{x} \ldots$ For example: $2 > \sqrt{2} > \sqrt[3]{2}$

○ **Region II**: A number $x$ in the region satisfies $0 < x < 1$

Higher the exponent of $x$, smaller is the value of the term and vice-versa.
Thus, we have:
$x > x^2 > x^3 \ldots$ For example: $\dfrac{1}{2} > \left(\dfrac{1}{2}\right)^2 > \left(\dfrac{1}{2}\right)^3$

$x < \sqrt{x} < \sqrt[3]{x} \ldots$ For example: $\dfrac{1}{2} < \sqrt{\dfrac{1}{2}} < \sqrt[3]{\dfrac{1}{2}}$

○ **Region III**: A number $x$ in the region satisfies $-1 < x < 0$

- For odd exponents (the values are always negative):
  Higher the exponent of $x$, higher is the value of the term and vice versa.
  Thus, we have:
  $x < x^3 < x^5 \ldots$ For example: $-\dfrac{1}{2} < \left(-\dfrac{1}{2}\right)^3 < \left(-\dfrac{1}{2}\right)^5$

  $x > \sqrt[3]{x} > \sqrt[5]{x} \ldots$ For example: $-\dfrac{1}{2} > \sqrt[3]{-\dfrac{1}{2}} > \sqrt[5]{-\dfrac{1}{2}}$

- For even exponents (the values are always positive):
  Higher the exponent of $x$, smaller is the value of the term and vice versa.
  Thus, we have:
  $x^2 > x^4 > x^6 \ldots$ For example: $\left(-\dfrac{1}{2}\right)^2 > \left(-\dfrac{1}{2}\right)^4 > \left(-\dfrac{1}{2}\right)^6$

  (Note: Square roots and fourth roots, etc. are not possible for negative numbers)

  An even exponent results in a positive value, which will always be greater than the value resulting from an odd exponent, which is always negative.

- ○ **Region IV**: A number $x$ in the region satisfies $-\infty < x < -1$
  - • For odd exponents (the values are always negative):
    Higher the exponent of $x$, smaller is the value of the term and vice versa.

    Thus, we have:

    $x > x^3 > x^5 \dots$ For example: $-2 > (-2)^3 > (-2)^5$

    $x < \sqrt[3]{x} < \sqrt[5]{x} \dots$ For example: $-2 < \sqrt[3]{-2} < \sqrt[5]{-2}$

  - • For even exponents (the values are always positive):
    Higher the exponent of $x$, higher is the value of the term and vice versa.

    Thus, we have:

    $x^2 < x^4 < x^6 \dots$ For example: $(-2)^2 < (-2)^4 < (-2)^6$

    (Note: Square roots and fourth roots, etc. are not possible for negative numbers)

    An even exponent results in a positive value, which will always be greater than the value resulting from an odd exponent, which is always negative.

(2) **Quadratic inequalities**: We have the following two rules:

  - ○ $x^2 < k^2 \Rightarrow -k < x < k$
  - ○ $x^2 > k^2 \Rightarrow x < -k$ OR $x > k$

    A simple way to remember this is to take square root and add $\pm$ to the $x$ term:

    - ○ $x^2 < k^2 \Rightarrow \pm x < k \Rightarrow x < k$ or $x > -k \Rightarrow -k < x < k$

    - ○ $x^2 > k^2 \Rightarrow \pm x > k \Rightarrow x > k$ or $x < -k$

Any quadratic can be converted to one of the above two forms.

Let us take an example:

$x^2 - 8x + 12 < 0$

$\Rightarrow (x^2 - 2 \times x \times 4 + 4^2) - 4^2 + 12 < 0$

$\Rightarrow (x - 4)^2 < 4$

$\Rightarrow -2 < x - 4 < 2$

$\Rightarrow 2 < x < 6$

Alternately, we can use the rules below: If $(x - k)$ and $(x - m)$ are the factors of a quadratic, and $k > m$, we have:

- $(x - k)(x - m) > 0 => x > k$ OR $x < m$

   Thus, $x$ is greater than the greatest root OR smaller than the smallest root.

- $(x - k)(x - m) < 0 => m < x < k$

   Thus, $x$ lies between the two roots.

   Let us take an example:

   $x^2 - 8x + 12 < 0$

   $=> (x - 2)(x - 6) < 0$

   Since the roots are 2 and 6, with 6 being the greater root, we have:

   $=> 2 < x < 6$

(3) **Other Inequalities:**

- For any two positive numbers $a$ and $b$, we always have:
  $$\frac{(a + b)}{2} \geq \sqrt{ab}$$

- For a given sum of two or more quantities, the product of the quantities is maximized if the quantities are made equal.

Similarly, for a given product of two or more quantities, the sum of the quantities is minimized if the quantities are made equal.

Let us take a few examples:

- What is the maximum value of $a \times b$ if $2a + 3b = 20$?

   Since $2a + 3b = 20$, the product $2a \times 3b$ would be maximized if $2a = 3b$
   $=> 2a + 2a = 20 => a = 5$
   $=> 2a = 3b = 10$
   Thus, the maximum value of $2a \times 3b = 10 \times 10 = 100$

   $=>$ The maximum value of $a \times b = \dfrac{(2a) \times (3b)}{6} = \dfrac{100}{6} = \dfrac{50}{3}$

- What is the minimum perimeter of a rectangle having an area of 100?

   Let the length and width of the rectangle be $l$ and $w$, respectively.
   Thus, the area of a rectangle $= l \times w = 100$

   We need to minimize the perimeter, i.e. $2(l + w)$. Thus, we need to minimize the value of $(l + w)$.

   The value of $(l + w)$ will be minimized if $l = w$

$=> l \times l = 100 => l = 10$

$=> l = w = 10$

Thus, minimum perimeter $= 2\,(10 + 10) = 40$.

**Additional solved problems:**

(1) Which of the following is true about $x$ if $x^2 > x > x^3$?

    **(A)** $x > 1$

    **(B)** $0 < x < 1$

    **(C)** $-1 < x < 0$

    **(D)** $x < -1$

Explanation:

We know that there are four major regions on the number line:

    I. $x > 1$

    II. $0 < x < 1$

    III. $-1 < x < 0$

    IV. $x < -1$

Let us pick 1 number from each region and check whether it satisfies the given inequality:

- $x = 2 : 2^2 > 2 \ngtr 2^3$
- $x = \dfrac{1}{2} : \left(\dfrac{1}{2}\right)^2 \ngtr \dfrac{1}{2} > \left(\dfrac{1}{2}\right)^3$
- $x = -\dfrac{1}{2} : \left(-\dfrac{1}{2}\right)^2 > -\dfrac{1}{2} \ngtr \left(-\dfrac{1}{2}\right)^3$
- $x = -2 : (-2)^2 > -2 > (-2)^3$ – Satisfies

Hence, correct answer is option D.

**Alternate approach:**

Since $x^2$ is greater than both $x$, a term with a lower exponent and $x^3$, a term with a higher exponent, the value of $x$ must be negative.

Since $x$, a term with a smaller odd exponent, is greater than $x^3$, a term with a higher odd exponent, the value of $x$ must be less than $-1$.

## 3.3   Functions and graphs of functions

**Domain and Range:**

The Domain refers to the set of values of $x$ that can be used in the function.

The Range refers to the set of values of $f(x)$ obtained using the above values of $x$.

Let us take an example:

$f(x) = x^2 - 1$

Let the set of values of $x$ to be used be $\{-1, 0, 1\}$.

Thus, we have:

- $f(-1) = (-1)^2 - 1 = 0$
- $f(0) = 0^2 - 1 = -1$
- $f(1) = 1^2 - 1 = 0$

Here, Domain = $\{-1, 0, 1\}$ and Range = $\{-1, 0\}$

To determine the Domain for a function, two things need to be considered:

- For any term under a square-root or fourth-root, etc., the term should be non-negative.
  For example: $f(x) = \sqrt{x - 1}$
  We have: $x - 1 \geq 0 \Rightarrow x \geq 1$
  Thus, the Domain is: $1 \leq x < \infty$

- For any term in the denominator, the term must be non-zero.
  For example: $f(x) = \dfrac{2x}{x - 3}$
  We have: $x - 3 \neq 0 \Rightarrow x \neq 3$
  Thus, the Domain is: $x$ is any real number except 3
  $\Rightarrow -\infty < x < 3$ OR $3 < x < \infty$

Let us take an example:

$f(x) = \dfrac{x + 3}{\sqrt{2x - 4} - 4}$

Thus, we have:

- $2x - 4 \geq 0 \Rightarrow x \geq 2 \ldots (i)$
- $\sqrt{2x - 4} - 4 \neq 0 \Rightarrow \sqrt{2x - 4} \neq 4 \Rightarrow 2x - 4 \neq 16 \Rightarrow x \neq 10 \ldots (ii)$

Thus, the Domain: $2 \le x < 10$ OR $10 < x < \infty$

Note: The radical symbol for square root only gives the positive square root, i.e. $\sqrt{4} = 2$, not $\pm 2$.

**Composite functions:**

For any two functions $f(x)$ and $g(x)$, the functions defined as $f(f(x))$, $f(g(x))$, $g(g(x))$ and $g(f(x))$ are composite functions.

Let us take an example:

$f(x) = 2x + 1$ and $g(x) = x^2 - 1$

Thus, we have:

- $f(f(x)) = 2(f(x)) + 1 = 2(2x + 1) + 1 = 4x + 3$
- $f(g(x)) = 2(g(x)) + 1 = 2(x^2 - 1) + 1 = 2x^2 - 1$
- $g(g(x)) = (g(x))^2 - 1 = (x^2 - 1)^2 - 1 = x^4 - 2x^2$
- $g(f(x)) = (f(x))^2 - 1 = (2x + 1)^2 - 1 = 4x^2 + 4x$

**Special case in a composite function:**

If $f(x)$ and $g(x)$ are two functions and it is observed that $f(g(x)) = g(f(x)) = x$, we have:

Input $(a)$ $\Longrightarrow$ $f(x)$ $\Longrightarrow$ Output $(b)$     Input $(b)$ $\Longrightarrow$ $g(x)$ $\Longrightarrow$ Output $(a)$

Thus, we have:

If $f(a) = b \Rightarrow g(b) = a$

Note: Such functions $f(x)$ and $g(x)$ are inverse functions of one another.

Let us take an example:

If $f(x) = (x + 1)^3 - 1$ and $g(x) = \sqrt[3]{x + 1} - k$, such that $f(g(x)) = g(f(x))$, what is the value of $k$?

The normal way of solving, by evaluating the composite functions $f(g(x))$ and $g(f(x))$, is complicated. Instead, we use the above method:

$f(1) = (1 + 1)^3 - 1 = 7$

$\Rightarrow g(7) = 1$

$$=> \sqrt[3]{7+1} - k = 1 => 2 - k = 1$$

$$=> k = 1$$

**Periodic function:**

A function $f(x)$ is periodic if there exists a number $n$ so that $f(x + n) = f(x)$ for all $x$. Here, $n$ is the period of the function.

Let us take an example:

If $f(x + 3) = f(x + 2) - f(x + 1)$, what is the value of $n$ if $f(1) = -f(1 + n)$?

We have: $f(x + 3) = f(x + 2) - f(x + 1)$

Substituting different values of $x$:

- $x = 0 : f(3) = f(2) - f(1) \ldots (i)$
- $x = 1 : f(4) = f(3) - f(2) \ldots (ii)$

Adding (i) and (ii):

$$f(3) + f(4) = f(3) - f(1)$$

$$=> f(1) = -f(4)$$

$$=> f(1) = -f(1 + 3)$$

$$=> n = 3$$

**Piece-wise functions:**

Functions which have different expressions over different values of $x$ are piece-wise functions. Some examples are shown below:

(2) **Greatest Integer Function**: $f(x) = [x]$: It is a function that returns the greatest integer less than or equal to $x$. Thus, we have:

- $[1.23]$: Greatest integer less than or equal to 1.23, i.e. the greatest integer among 1, 0, $-1$, $-2$, $\cdots$ = 1
- $[1]$: Greatest integer less than or equal to 1, i.e. the greatest integer among 1, 0, $-1$, $-2$, $\cdots$ = 1
- $[-1.23]$: Greatest integer less than or equal to $-1.23$, i.e. the greatest integer among $-2$, $-3$, $-4$, $\cdots$ = $-2$
- $[-1]$: Greatest integer less than or equal to $-1$, i.e. the greatest integer among $-1$, $-2$, $-3$, $-4$, $\cdots$ = $-1$

(3) **Least Integer Function:** $f(x) = \{x\}$: It is a function that returns the least integer greater than or equal to $x$. Thus, we have:

   ○ $\{1.23\}$: The least integer greater than or equal to 1.23, i.e. the least integer among 2, 3, 4, $\cdots$ = 2

   ○ $\{1\}$: The least integer greater than or equal to 1, i.e. the least integer among 1, 2, 3, 4, $\cdots$ = 1

   ○ $\{-1.23\}$: The least integer greater than or equal to $-1.23$, i.e. the least integer among $-1$, 0, 1, 2, $\cdots$ = $-1$

   ○ $\{-1\}$: The least integer greater than or equal to $-1$, i.e. the least integer among $-1$, 0, 1, 2, $\cdots$ = $-1$

## Properties of graphs of functions:

- The graph of $f(x+p)$ is obtained by shifting the graph of $f(x)$ by $p$ units left
- The graph of $f(x-p)$ is obtained by shifting the graph of $f(x)$ by $p$ units right
- The graph of $f(x) + p$ is obtained by shifting the graph of $f(x)$ by $p$ units up
- The graph of $f(x) - p$ is obtained by shifting the graph of $f(x)$ by $p$ units down
- The graph of $f(-x)$ is obtained by reflecting the graph of $f(x)$ about the Y-axis
- The graph of $-f(x)$ is obtained by reflecting the graph of $f(x)$ about the X-axis

## Graphs of some quadratic functions:

- $f(x) = x^2$:

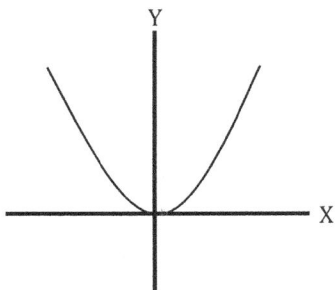

- $f(x) = x^2 + 1$:

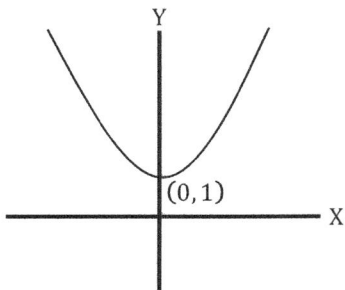

- $f(x) = (x-1)^2$:

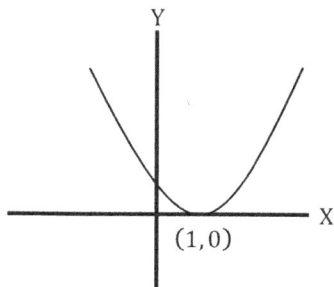

(1,0)

**Additional solved problems:**

(1) Are the following functions the same?

    **(A)** $f(x) = x^x$

    **(B)** $g(x) = x \times x \times x \times x \times \cdots \times x$ ($x$ times)

Explanation:

    **(A)** We have $f(x) = x^x$

    For example:

    If $x = 3 \Rightarrow f(x) = 3^3 = 27$

    If $x = -1 \Rightarrow f(-1) = (-1)^{-1} = -1$

    If $x = \dfrac{1}{2} \Rightarrow f\left(\dfrac{1}{2}\right) = \left(\dfrac{1}{2}\right)^{\frac{1}{2}} = \dfrac{1}{\sqrt{2}} = \approx \dfrac{1}{1.4} = 0.71$

    Thus, $f(x) = x^x$ is valid for all real values of $x$ except for reciprocals of negative even numbers like $x = -\dfrac{1}{2}$. (since, if $x = -\dfrac{1}{2} \Rightarrow x^x = \left(-\dfrac{1}{2}\right)^{\left(-\frac{1}{2}\right)} = \dfrac{1}{\left(-\frac{1}{2}\right)^{\left(\frac{1}{2}\right)}}$, an imaginary number.

    **(B)** We have: $g(x) = x \times x \times x \times x \times x \times \cdots \times x$ ($x$ times)

    If $x$ is multiplied for $x$ times, the result obtained is $x^x$.

    Thus, apparently, $f(x)$ and $g(x)$ appear to be identical.

    However, we are multiplying $x$ for $x$ times, which makes sense only when $x$ is a positive integer. (Multiplying $\dfrac{1}{2}$ for $\dfrac{1}{2}$ times or multiplying $-1$ for $-1$ times makes no sense)

For example:

$g(3) = 3 \times 3 \times 3$ (3 is multiplied for 3 times)

$= 27$

Thus, $g(x)$ is valid only for positive integer values of $x$.

Thus, $f(x)$ is not the same as $g(x)$.

(2) If (2, 1) are the coordinates of a point on the graph of $f(x)$, what would be the coordinates of that point for the function $-f(x) + 1$?

Explanation:

To modify $f(x)$ to $-f(x) + 1$, we follow the following steps:

- $f(x) \rightarrow -f(x)$: The graph is reflected about the X-axis. Thus, the Y-coordinate of the point would be negated.
  Thus, the coordinates of $-f(x) = (2, -1)$

- $-f(x) \rightarrow -f(x) + 1$: The graph is shifted 'up' by 1 unit. Thus, the Y-coordinate of th point would increase by '1'.
  Thus, the final coordinates of $-f(x) + 1 = (2, -1 + 1) = (2, 0)$

(3) If (2, 1) are the coordinates of a point on the graph of $f(x)$, what would be the coordinates of that point for the function $f(x - 1)$?

Explanation:

We need to modify $f(x) \rightarrow f(x - 1)$, i.e. the graph should shift one unit left, hence, value of $x$ should decrease by 1. Thus, (2, 1) gets modified to (1, 1).

**Alternate approach:**

If (2, 1) are the coordinates of a point on the graph of $f(x)$, what would be the coordinates of that point for the function $2f(-3x - 1) + 1$? The new $x$ value is obtained by solving: $-3x - 1 = 2 \Rightarrow x = -1$. The new $y$ value is obtained by substituting the original $y$ value in the new function: $2(1) + 1 = 3$. Thus, the coordinates are: $(-1, 3)$.

In the next chapter, you will find exam-like questions. Best of luck!

# Chapter 4

# Practice Questions

**1.** If $p\left(1 + r^2\right)^3 = q$, and $r$ is a positive quantity, which of the following gives the correct relation of $r$ in terms of $p$ and $q$? [Without calculator]

(A) $r = \left\{ \left(\dfrac{p}{q}\right)^{\frac{1}{3}} - 1 \right\}^{\frac{1}{2}}$

(B) $r = \left\{ \left(\dfrac{p}{q}\right)^{\frac{1}{2}} - 1 \right\}^{\frac{1}{3}}$

(C) $r = \left\{ \left(\dfrac{q}{p}\right)^{\frac{1}{3}} - 1 \right\}^{\frac{1}{2}}$

(D) $r = \left\{ \left(\dfrac{q}{p}\right)^{\frac{1}{2}} - 1 \right\}^{\frac{1}{3}}$

*Solve yourself:*

**2.** Which of the following shows the equation of a circle having center at $(-2,\ 5)$ and radius double that of the circle $x^2 - 2x + y^2 + 4y = 4$? [Without calculator]

(A) $x^2 - 4x + y^2 + 10y = 7$

(B) $x^2 + 4x + y^2 - 10y = 7$

(C) $x^2 - 4x + y^2 + 10y = 36$

(D) $x^2 + 4x + y^2 + 10y = 36$

*Solve yourself:*

**3.** A factory manufactures $s$ units of a product X whose average manufacturing cost per unit, in dollars, is a function of $s$, given as $f(s) = 3 + 2.5s$. If each item is sold at a fixed price of $\$p$, which of the following represents the condition for a profit by selling all $s$ units? [Without calculator]

(A) $3s + 2.5s - ps > 0$

(B) $3 + 2.5s^2 - ps > 0$

(C) $3 + 2.5s^2 - p < 0$

(D) $3s + 2.5s^2 - ps < 0$

*Solve yourself:*

4.  A man saves \$$x$ in a particular month. Thereafter, each month, he saves \$$y$ more than what he saved the previous month. If he saved \$$z$ in the tenth month from the beginning, what is the relation between $x$, $y$ and $z$? [Without calculator]

    **(A)**  $y = \dfrac{z + x}{10}$

    **(B)**  $y = \dfrac{z + x}{9}$

    **(C)**  $y = \dfrac{z - x}{10}$

    **(D)**  $y = \dfrac{z - x}{9}$

    *Solve yourself:*

5.  In a bacteria sample having $n$ bacteria, it was found that each bacterium divides into two identical cells after 20 minutes. After $t$ hours, the number of bacteria was found to be $m$. If $t$ is an integer, which of the following represents the relation between $m$, $n$ and $t$? [Without calculator]

    **(A)**  $n = m \times 2^{t}$

    **(B)**  $n = m \times 2^{3t}$

    **(C)**  $n = m \times 2^{-3t}$

    **(D)**  $n = m \times 2^{-t}$

    *Solve yourself:*

6.  **Grid-In:**

    The distance, in miles, covered by a rocket in $t$ seconds after its launch is given by the function $d(t) = 3t^{2}$. What is the distance, in miles, covered by the rocket in the $5^{\text{th}}$ second after its launch? [Without calculator]

*Solve yourself:*

7. **Grid-In:**

   If the roots of the equation $x^2 - 2x - 15 = 0$ are $a$ and $b$, where $a > b$, what is the value of $a + b^2$? [Without calculator]

   *Solve yourself:*

8. If the roots of the equation $x^2 - (b + c)x + bc = 0$ are equal in magnitude and opposite in sign, which of the following statements are true? [Without calculator]

   (A)  $b = -c$

   (B)  $b = c$

   (C)  $b = c^2$

   (D)  $b^2 = c$

   *Solve yourself:*

9. If $a$ and $b$ are the roots of $x^2 - 10x + 16 = 0$, what is the equation whose roots are given by $(a + b)^2$ and $(a - b)^2$? [Without calculator]

   (A)  $x^2 - 16x - 60 = 0$

   (B)  $x^2 + 4x + 60 = 0$

   (C)  $x^2 - 3600x + 136 = 0$

   (D)  $x^2 - 136x + 3600 = 0$

   *Solve yourself:*

10. **Grid-In:**

   If $x^2 + 3x - 40 = 0$ and $y^2 + 4y - 60 = 0$, what is the maximum possible value of $\frac{x}{y}$? [With calculator]

   *Solve yourself:*

11. **Grid-In:**

   If both roots of the quadratic equation $x^2 + px + 6 = 0$ are integers, how many possible values of $p$ exist? [Without calculator]

   *Solve yourself:*

12. **Grid-In:**

   In the quadratic equation $x^2 + (a + 1)x + (a + 5) = 0$, if the sum of the roots is $-5$, what is the product of the roots? [Without calculator]

   *Solve yourself:*

13. If $9^x - 3^{x+1} - 54 = 0$, what is the value of $9^x$? [With calculator]

   **(A)** $-6$
   **(B)** $2$
   **(C)** $9$
   **(D)** $81$

   *Solve yourself:*

14. If $x^2 - 2x - 24 < 0$, how many integer values of $x$ are possible? [Without calculator]

    **(A)** Six

    **(B)** Eight

    **(C)** Nine

    **(D)** Eleven

    *Solve yourself:*

15. Which of the following statements is true regarding the expression $f(x) = x^2 - 6x + 12$?
[With calculator]

    **(A)** The expression has a least value of 3

    **(B)** The value of the expression is always negative for any value of $x$

    **(C)** The roots of $f(x) = 0$ are real

    **(D)** None of the above

    *Solve yourself:*

16. **Grid-In:**

    A ball is thrown upwards from a height of 10 feet above the ground level. The height, in feet, of the ball above the ground $t$ seconds after being thrown upwards is given by $h(t) = -t^2 + 8t + 10$. How many seconds after being thrown upwards will the ball reach its maximum height above the ground level? [Without calculator]

    *Solve yourself:*

17. **Grid-In:**

    A ball is thrown upwards from a particular height above the ground level. The height, in feet, of the ball above the ground after time $x$ seconds from when it was thrown is given by the expression $h(t) = -t^2 + 4t + 6$. What is the maximum height the ball will reach above the ground level? [Without calculator]

*Solve yourself:*

18.  Ross throws a ball upwards from a certain height above the ground level. The height, in feet, of the ball above the ground after time $t$ seconds from when the ball was thrown is given by the expression $h(t) = -(t - p)^2 + q$. The ball reaches a maximum height of 16 feet after 3 seconds. How many seconds after being thrown upwards will the ball reach the ground level? [Without calculator]

   **(A)**  4

   **(B)**  7

   **(C)**  10

   **(D)**  12

   *Solve yourself:*

19.  If $\sqrt{x + 2} + \sqrt{x - 1} = 3$, what is the value of $x^2$? [With calculator]

   **(A)**  2

   **(B)**  4

   **(C)**  8

   **(D)**  16

   *Solve yourself:*

20.  If the roots of the equation $3x^2 + 4x + 1 = 0$ are $p$ and $q$, what is the value of $(3 - 2p)(2q - 3)$? [With calculator]

   **(A)**  $\dfrac{32}{3}$

   **(B)**  $-\dfrac{12}{5}$

   **(C)**  $-\dfrac{55}{3}$

(D)   $-\dfrac{67}{3}$

   *Solve yourself:*

21.   A quadratic equation $x^2+6x+8 = 0$ has two roots $p$ and $q$ while another equation $ax^2+bx+c = 0$ has the roots $\frac{1}{p}$ and $\frac{1}{q}$. If $a > 0$ and $a$, $b$ and c are all integers, what is the least possible value of $c$? [Without calculator]

   (A)   $-8$

   (B)   $-1$

   (C)   $1$

   (D)   $8$

   *Solve yourself:*

22.   If $x^2 - 5x + 6 = 0$ and $y^2 + 6y - 7 = 0$, which of the following is correct? [Without calculator]

   (A)   $x > y$

   (B)   $x \geq y$

   (C)   $y \geq x$

   (D)   $y > x$

   *Solve yourself:*

23.   **Grid-In:**

   If the breadth of a rectangle is 6 cm less than the length and the area of the rectangle is 16 square cm, what is the perimeter of the rectangle in centimeter? [Without calculator]

*Solve yourself:*

**24.**  $f(x) = x^2 + 6x + 8$ and $h(x) = 32 + 4x$. At how many points do the graphs of the two functions intersect? [Without calculator]

(A)  None

(B)  One

(C)  Two

(D)  Three

*Solve yourself:*

**25.**  If the equation $x - 3 = \sqrt{x^2 - 3}$ has an extraneous solution, what is the extraneous solution? [Without calculator]

(A)  $-1$

(B)  1

(C)  2

(D)  3

*Solve yourself:*

**26.  Grid-In:**

The sum of the squares of two consecutive positive odd numbers is 74. What is the sum of the digits of the two numbers? [Without calculator]

*Solve yourself:*

**27.** A local club has a rectangular football field whose length is 16 meters more than its breadth. There is a running track of width 2 meters around all the sides of the field. If the area of the track is $\frac{1}{3}$ of the football field, what is the length of the football field (in meters)? [Without calculator]

**(A)** 18

**(B)** 20

**(C)** 24

**(D)** 36

*Solve yourself:*

**28.** Peter bought some oranges from the market for \$144. He later calculated that if each orange had cost \$2 less, he would have been able to buy exactly 12 more oranges with the same sum. What was the number of oranges bought by Peter? [Without calculator]

**(A)** 12

**(B)** 18

**(C)** 24

**(D)** 26

*Solve yourself:*

**29.** A manufacturer produces speakers, the production cost for which is given by the function $f(n) = n^2 + 14n$, where $n$ is the number, in millions, of speakers produced, while the warehousing cost is given by the function $g(n) = n^2 + 2n$. If the manufacturer sells each speaker for \$40, which of the following production numbers will maximize his profit? [Without calculator]

**(A)** $n = 6$

**(B)** $n = 7$

**(C)** $n = 8$

**(D)** $n = 10$

*Solve yourself:*

**30.** A man drove at a uniform speed of $x$ miles per hour and reached his destination in $(x + 2)$ hours. Had he driven at $y$ more miles per hour, where $\neq 0$, , he would have reached his destination in $\frac{3y}{4}$ hours less time. Which of the following is the correct relation between $x$ and $y$?  [Without calculator]

    **(A)**   $x = 8y - 3$

    **(B)**   $x = 8y + 3$

    **(C)**   $x = 3y - 8$

    **(D)**   $x = 8 - 3y$

    *Solve yourself:*

**31.** If $ax^2 - 36 = 0$ has integer roots less than 2, how many integer values of $a$ exist?  [Without calculator]

    **(A)**   One

    **(B)**   Two

    **(C)**   Three

    **(D)**   More than three

    *Solve yourself:*

**32.** If $\frac{1}{2}\left(\frac{1}{x-4}\right)(x^2 - 16) = \left(1 + \frac{4}{x-4}\right)(x - 4)$, how many values of $x$ exist?  [Without calculator]

    **(A)**   None

    **(B)**   One

    **(C)**   Two

    **(D)**   Three

    *Solve yourself:*

**33.** A man deposits \$10 in a bank. The bank gives interest at the rate of $r\%$ every 3 years, compounded triennially (computed once in every three years). What will be the amount of money in the bank after $n$ years?  [Without calculator]

(A)  $\${10(1 + \frac{r}{100})^{3n}}$

(B)  $\${10(1 + \frac{r}{100})^{(\frac{n}{3})}}$

(C)  $\${10(1 + \frac{r}{300})^{n}}$

(D)  $\${10(1 + \frac{r}{300})^{3n}}$

*Solve yourself:*

34.  **Grid-In:**

At time $t = 0$ hours, two strains of bacteria had 1024 and 64 bacteria respectively. It was observed that the first strain doubled every 9 hours, while the second strain doubled every 3 hours. In how many hours would the strains have the same number of bacteria? [With calculator]

*Solve yourself:*

35.  How many positive numbers exist such that the difference between the square of the number and the number is 12? [With calculator]

(A)  None

(B)  One

(C)  Two

(D)  Three

*Solve yourself:*

36.  What is the value of $(a + b)$ if the equations $x^2 - 6ax + 12 = 0$ and $x^2 - 4x + 9b = 0$ have both roots common? [Without calculator]

(A)  1

**(B)** $\frac{2}{3}$

**(C)** $\frac{4}{3}$

**(D)** 2

*Solve yourself:*

**37.** What is the sum of all possible values of $x$ if $(x-3)^{(x-6)} = 1$? [Without calculator]

**(A)** 6

**(B)** 8

**(C)** 10

**(D)** 12

*Solve yourself:*

**38.** For how many positive integer values of $x$ less than 4 is $(x-1)(x+2) = 2^x$? [With calculator]

**(A)** None

**(B)** One

**(C)** Two

**(D)** Three

*Solve yourself:*

**39.** If $4^{(x^2-2x)} = 8^2$, how many values of $x$ exist? [Without calculator]

**(A)** None

**(B)** One

**(C)** Two

**(D)** Infinitely many

**40.  Grid-In:**

What is the sum of all possible real roots of the equation: $x^3 - 3x^2 + 4x - 12 = 0$? [Without calculator]

*Solve yourself:*

**41.**  The distance, in feet, covered by a ball in $t$ seconds after being dropped from the top of a building is given by $9t^2$. If the distance covered by the ball in the $t^{\text{th}}$ second after being dropped is $h$ feet, which of the following is the correct expression of $t$ in terms of $h$? [Without calculator]

(A)  $\frac{1}{2}(h + 9)$

(B)  $\frac{1}{2}\left(\frac{h}{9} - 1\right)$

(C)  $\frac{1}{2}\left(\frac{h}{9} + 1\right)$

(D)  $2\left(\frac{h}{9} + 1\right)$

*Solve yourself:*

**42.  Grid-In:**

If one of the solutions of $x^2 - px + 12 = 0$ is $x = 3$, what is the value of $p$? [Without calculator]

*Solve yourself:*

**43.**  The curve $y = x^2 + 3x + 1$ intersects the line $y = x + 1$ at two points. What is the value of the $y$ coordinate of the point closer to the X-axis? [Without calculator]

(A)  $-3$

(B)  $-2$

(C)  $0$

(D)  $1$

*Solve yourself:*

**44.** For $f(x) = x^2 + bx + c$, $f(1) = 2$. If $f(2) = 0$, what is the value of $f(0)$? [Without calculator]

    **(A)** $-6$

    **(B)** $-5$

    **(C)** $5$

    **(D)** $6$

*Solve yourself:*

**45.** If $f(x) = x^3 - kx + 2$ and $f(-2) = f(2)$, what is the value of $k$? [Without calculator]

    **(A)** $0$

    **(B)** $1$

    **(C)** $2$

    **(D)** $4$

*Solve yourself:*

**46. Grid-In:**

If $f(x) = \sqrt{9 - x^2}$, for how many integer values of $x$ would the value of $f(x)$ be real? [Without calculator]

*Solve yourself:*

**47.** The function $f(x)$ is defined according to the given table:

| $x$ | $f(x)$ |
|-----|--------|
| 1   | 2      |
| 2   | 5      |
| 3   | 8      |
| 4   | 11     |

Which of the following is a correct representation of the function $f(x)$? [Without calculator]

**(A)** $x^2 + 1$

**(B)** $3x - 1$

**(C)** $x + 4$

**(D)** $x^3 + 1$

*Solve yourself:*

**48.** Functions $f(x)$ and $g(x)$ are defined such that their values for different values of $x$ are as shown:

| $x$ | $f(x)$ | $g(x)$ |
|-----|--------|--------|
| 1   | 5      | 3      |
| 2   | 4      | 4      |
| 3   | 3      | 5      |
| 4   | 2      | 6      |
| 5   | 1      | 7      |

What is the value of $f(g(1)) + g(f(1))$? [Without calculator]

**(A)** 2

**(B)** 3

**(C)** 7

**(D)** 10

*Solve yourself:*

**49.** If $f(x) = |x| + x$ and $g(x) + f(x) = 2x$, what is the value of $g(-2)$? [Without calculator]

**(A)** $-8$

**(B)**   −4

**(C)**   0

**(D)**   8

*Solve yourself:*

**50.**   A quadratic function $f(x)$ intersects the X-axis at $(1, 0)$ and $(5, 0)$. If $f(2) = 3$, what is the value of $f(4)$? [With calculator]

**(A)**   −1

**(B)**   3

**(C)**   4

**(D)**   6

*Solve yourself:*

**51.**   For all integer values of $x$, let $f(x) = \dfrac{1}{\sqrt{1 - x^2} - 1}$. Which of the following options correctly represents the values of $x$ for which $f(x)$ is defined? [Without calculator]

**(A)**   $\{0\}$

**(B)**   $\{0, 1\}$

**(C)**   $\{-1, 1\}$

**(D)**   $\{-1, 0, 1\}$

*Solve yourself:*

**52.  Grid-In:**

If $f(x) = ax^2 + x$ such that $f(1) = f(0) + 2$, what is the value of $f(2)$? [Without calculator]

*Solve yourself:*

**53.**  If $x = \sqrt{3} - 1$, what is the value of $(x^2 + 2x)$? [Without calculator]

(A)  $-2$

(B)  $-\sqrt{3}$

(C)  $\sqrt{3}$

(D)  $2$

*Solve yourself:*

**54.**  If $a$ and $b$ are non-zero integers such that $a^2 + b^2 - 4a - 2b = 0$ and $|a - b| = 0$, what is the value of $(a + b)$? [Without calculator]

(A)  $-3$

(B)  $0$

(C)  $3$

(D)  $6$

*Solve yourself:*

**55.**  If $x, y$ and $z$ are positive integers with $x + y = 4$ and $z = x^2 + y^2$, what is the minimum value of $z$? [Without calculator]

(A)  $4$

(B)  $6$

(C)  $8$

(D)  $10$

*Solve yourself:*

**56.** If $x$ and $y$ are positive integers such that $2x + y = 8$ and $z = x^2 - y^2$, what is the maximum value of $z$? [Without calculator]

**(A)** 0

**(B)** 3

**(C)** 5

**(D)** 7

*Solve yourself:*

**57.** For all integers $x > 1$, let $f(x)$ be defined as $f(x) = (-1)^x \times f(x - 1)$. If $f(1) = 1$, what is the value of $f(7)$? [Without calculator]

**(A)** $-3$

**(B)** $-1$

**(C)** 1

**(D)** 3

*Solve yourself:*

**58.**

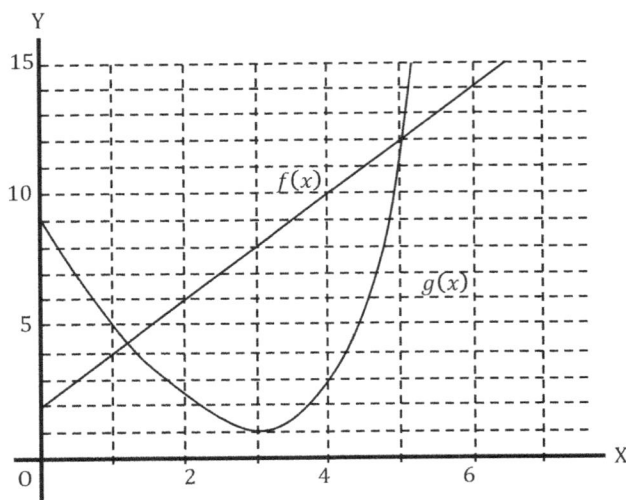

The given graph represents two functions $f(x)$ and $g(x)$. If $f(1) = k$, which of the following is the value of $g(k)$? [Without calculator]

**(A)**   0

**(B)**   1

**(C)**   2

**(D)**   3

*Solve yourself:*

**59.**   If $a > 1$, which of the following is an equivalent expression of $\left( \dfrac{1}{\sqrt{a+1} + \sqrt{a}} \right)$? [Without calculator]

**(A)**   $\sqrt{a-1} + \sqrt{a}$

**(B)**   $\sqrt{a-1} - \sqrt{a}$

**(C)**   $\sqrt{a+1} - \sqrt{a}$

**(D)**   $\sqrt{a+1} + \sqrt{a}$

*Solve yourself:*

**60.** For which of the following functions is $f(a + 1) = f(a) \times f(1)$ for all values of $a$? [Without calculator]

    **(A)** $f(x) = x + 2$

    **(B)** $f(x) = x^2$

    **(C)** $f(x) = 2x$

    **(D)** $f(x) = 2^x$

    *Solve yourself:*

**61.** **Grid-In:**

$f(x) = \dfrac{x - k}{5}$ and $g(x) = 5x + 1$. If $f(g(x)) = x$, what is the value of $k$? [Without calculator]

*Solve yourself:*

**62.** $f(x) = \dfrac{x - 1}{2x + k}$, where $k$ is a constant. If $f(f(x)) = x$, what is the value of $k$? **NC**

    **(A)** 3

    **(B)** 2

    **(C)** $-1$

    **(D)** $-2$

    *Solve yourself:*

**63.** **Grid-In:**

A function $f(x)$ is defined such that:

- $f(x) = f(x - 1) + 2$ if $x$ is prime
- $f(x) = f(x - 1) + 1$ if $x$ is non-prime

If $f(1) = 3$, what is the value of (5)? [Without calculator]

(A)   6

(B)   7

(C)   8

(D)   10

*Solve yourself:*

64.   If $f(x) = \dfrac{2^x + 1}{2^x}$, which of the following is correct? [Without calculator]

(A)   $f(-1) = f(1)$

(B)   $f(-1) = -f(1)$

(C)   $f(-1) = -f(-1)$

(D)   None of the above

*Solve yourself:*

65.   If $f(x) = ax^2 + b$ and $f(x+1) = f(x) + x + \frac{1}{2}$, for all values of $x$, what is the value of $a$?
[Without calculator]

(A)   $-2$

(B)   $-1$

(C)   $\frac{1}{2}$

(D)   1

*Solve yourself:*

66.   If $f(x) = 2^{x-1}$, what is the value of $\dfrac{f(1) \times f(2)}{f(3)}$? [Without calculator]

(A)   0.04

(B)   0.06

**(C)**   0.25

**(D)**   0.50

*Solve yourself:*

**67.**   $f(x) = x^5 - x^2$. Which of the following statements are true regarding the graph of $f(x)$?
[Without calculator]

    **I.**   $f(x)$ passes through the origin

    **II.**   $f(x)$ always lies above the X-axis

    **III.**   $f(x)$ is symmetric about the origin

**(A)**   Only I

**(B)**   Only II

**(C)**   Only III

**(D)**   I and III

*Solve yourself:*

**68.**   A manufacturer incurs production cost and transportation cost for manufacturing articles. The production cost, in dollars, for manufacturing $n$ articles is given by the function $f(n) = 120n - n^2$ while transportation cost, in dollars, is given by the function $g(n) = 60n - n^2$. If the manufacturer sells each article for \$50, which of the following represents the condition, in terms of $n$, for the manufacturer to make a profit? [Without calculator]

**(A)**   $n < 65$

**(B)**   $n \leq 65$

**(C)**   $n \geq 65$

**(D)**   $n > 65$

*Solve yourself:*

**69.** In the equation $x - 3 = \sqrt{x^2 - 15}$, what value of $x$, if it exists, is the extraneous solution? [Without calculator]

  **(A)** $-4$

  **(B)** $0$

  **(C)** $4$

  **(D)** There is no extraneous solution

  *Solve yourself:*

**70.** **Grid-In:**

  The sum of the squares of two consecutive positive odd numbers is 290. What is the number obtained by adding the sums of the digits of the two numbers? [Without calculator]

  *Solve yourself:*

**71.** What is the minimum integer value of $x$ for which $(0.25)^x > (0.125)^{2x-3}$? [Without calculator]

  **(A)** $1$

  **(B)** $2$

  **(C)** $3$

  **(D)** $4$

  *Solve yourself:*

**72.** If $x < y < -x$, which of the following must be true? [Without calculator]

  **(A)** $xy < 0$

  **(B)** $xy > 0$

  **(C)** $x^2y > 0$

  **(D)** $xy^2 < 0$

*Solve yourself:*

73.  If $y = x^2 - x + 1$, which of the following is true about $y$? [Without calculator]

   **(A)**   $y \geq 0$
   **(B)**   $y > 0$
   **(C)**   $y < x$
   **(D)**   $y > x$

   *Solve yourself:*

74.  If $-\frac{19}{5} = 3a - 1 = \frac{17}{3}$, how many integer values are possible for $(a + 1)$? [Without calculator]

   **(A)**   Three
   **(B)**   Four
   **(C)**   Five
   **(D)**   Seven

   *Solve yourself:*

75.  If $|x - 3| = 7$, how many integer values of $|x - 1|$ are possible? [Without calculator]

   **(A)**   Six
   **(B)**   Nine
   **(C)**   Ten
   **(D)**   Fifteen

   *Solve yourself:*

**76.**   A man puts $1000 in a bank which offers $r\%$ interest compounded annually. After 3 years, the amount of money in the bank is $P. Which of the following is the correct expression of $r$ in terms of $P$? [Without calculator]

   **(A)**   $100\left\{\dfrac{P\left(\frac{1}{3}\right)}{1000} - 1\right\}$

   **(B)**   $100\left\{\left(\dfrac{P}{1000}\right)^{(3)} - 1\right\}$

   **(C)**   $100\left\{\left(\dfrac{P}{1000}\right)^{\left(\frac{1}{3}\right)} - 1\right\}$

   **(D)**   $100\left\{\left(\dfrac{P}{1000}\right)^{\left(\frac{1}{3}\right)} + 1\right\}$

   *Solve yourself:*

**77.**   What is the sum of all possible integer values of $x$ if $(0.25)^x < 2^{(2-3x)}$ and $|x| < 3$? [Without calculator]

   **(A)**   $-2$

   **(B)**   $-1$

   **(C)**   $0$

   **(D)**   $1$

   *Solve yourself:*

**78.**

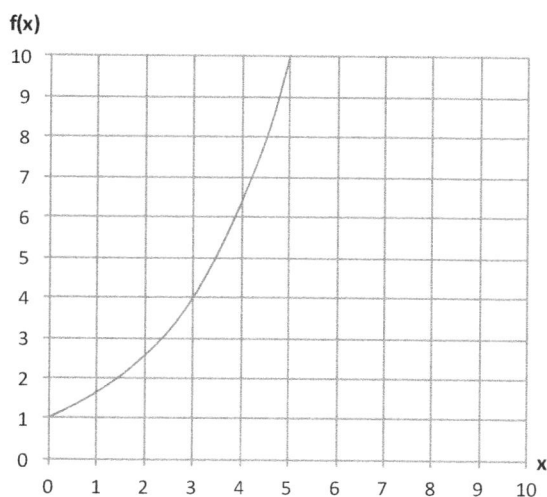

The graph is for the function $f(x) = p^x$. Which of the following options is correct? [Without calculator]

**(A)**  $0 < p < 1$

**(B)**  $1 < p < 2$

**(C)**  $p = 2$

**(D)**  $2 < p < 3$

*Solve yourself:*

**79.** A man travels a distance $d$ miles at a speed of $s$ miles per hour. Had he travelled the distance at $(s + 10)$ miles per hour, he would have reached his destination more than 1 hour earlier. Which of the following is a correct relation between $s$ and $d$? [Without calculator]

**(A)**  $ds > \frac{s}{10} + 10$

**(B)**  $ds > \frac{s}{10} - 1$

**(C)**  $\frac{1}{10}s(s + 10) < d$

**(D)**  $\frac{1}{10}s(s + 10) > d$

*Solve yourself:*

**80.** An athlete follows a strict training regimen – on the first day, he runs distance $d$ units; thereafter, each day, he increases the distance by 20%. If, on the final day of his regimen, he runs more than $D$ units, what is the relation between the number of days, $n$, for which he follows the training regimen, and the distances he ran on the first and last day? [Without calculator]

(A) $\left(\frac{D}{d}\right)^{(n-1)} > \frac{6}{5}$

(B) $\left(\frac{D}{d}\right)^{(n-1)} < \frac{6}{5}$

(C) $\left(\frac{D}{d}\right)^{\left(\frac{1}{n-1}\right)} > \frac{6}{5}$

(D) $\left(\frac{D}{d}\right)^{\left(\frac{1}{n-1}\right)} < \frac{6}{5}$

*Solve yourself:*

**81.** If $x^2 > x^7 > x$, which of the following statements must be correct? [Without calculator]

   **I.** $x^4 > x^5$

   **II.** $0 < x < 1$

   **III.** $-1 < x < 0$

(A) Only I

(B) Only II

(C) Only III

(D) Both I and III

*Solve yourself:*

**82.** If $a^5 b^4 c^3 d^6$ is negative, where $a, b, c, \& d$ are integers, which of the following must be correct? [Without calculator]

(A) $ab$ is positive

(B) $b^2 d$ is positive

(C) $b^3 c^2$ is positive

(D) $a^3 c^3$ is negative

*Solve yourself:*

**83.** Choose the correct option based on the relative values of $p, q, r$ and $s$ as shown in the figure:

[Without calculator]

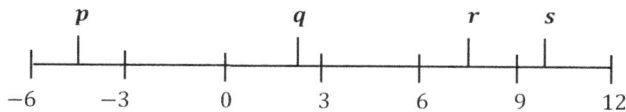

    **(A)** $ps > q^2$

    **(B)** $qr < s^2$

    **(C)** $pr > s^2$

    **(D)** $rs < p^3$

*Solve yourself:*

**84.** If $m = px + qy$ and $n = qx + py$, where $p \neq \pm q$, what is $x$ in terms of $m, n, p$ and $q$?

[Without calculator]

    **(A)** $x = \frac{mq - np}{q^2 - p^2}$

    **(B)** $x = \frac{mp - nq}{p^2 - q^2}$

    **(C)** $x = \frac{mq - np}{p^2 - q^2}$

    **(D)** $x = \frac{mp - nq}{q^2 - p^2}$

*Solve yourself:*

**85.** If $-4 = x = 8$ and $-8 = y = 16$, with both $x$ and $y$ being integers and $y \neq 0$, what is the difference between the maximum and minimum values of $\left(\frac{x}{y}\right)$? [Without calculator]

    **(A)** 0

          

(B)   $\dfrac{33}{4}$

(C)   $\dfrac{129}{16}$

(D)   16

*Solve yourself:*

86.   If $x > 4$ and $y > 8$, what is the smallest integer value of $(x + y)$? [Without calculator]

(A)   11

(B)   12

(C)   13

(D)   14

*Solve yourself:*

87.   The terms $A$, $B$, $C$ and $D$ are related by the equation: $A \times \sqrt[3]{C} = \frac{B \times \sqrt{D}}{5}$. What is the value of $C$ if $A = 5$, $B = 2$, and $D = 16$? [With calculator]

(A)   $\frac{8}{25}$

(B)   $\frac{64}{625}$

(C)   $\frac{512}{15625}$

(D)   $\frac{256}{15625}$

*Solve yourself:*

88.   The half-life of a substance is the number of seconds it takes for the mass of the substance to become half its original value. The initial weight of one such substance is 28 grams. If the half-life of the substance is 42 seconds, which of the following represents the mass of the substance after 210 seconds? [Without calculator]

(A)   $28 \times \left(\frac{1}{2}\right)^{109}$

**(B)** $28 \times \left(\frac{1}{2}\right)^{42}$

**(C)** $28 \times \left(\frac{1}{2}\right)^{5}$

**(D)** $28 \times \left(\frac{1}{2}\right)^{2}$

*Solve yourself:*

89. The force, $F$, between two bodies having mass $M$ and $m$, separated by a distance $D$ is given by the equation $F = \frac{GMm}{D^2}$, where $G$ is a constant. If the distance is doubled, and one of the masses is also doubled, what will be the effect on the force? [Without calculator]

    **(A)** The force is quadrupled

    **(B)** The force is doubled

    **(C)** The force remains unchanged

    **(D)** The force is halved

    *Solve yourself:*

90. A man types $x$ pages on the first day and thereafter every day he increases his typing speed by $n\%$ from the previous day till he completes the typing task, in a total of $D$ days. If he works for the same duration of time every day, which of the following represents the correct expression for $n$ in terms of $D$, $x$, and the number of pages, $p$, that he typed on the last day? [Without calculator]

    **(A)** $n = \left\{ \left(\frac{p}{x}\right)^{(D-1)} - 1 \right\} \times 100$

    **(B)** $n = \left\{ \left(\frac{p}{x}\right)^{(D)} - 1 \right\} \times 100$

    **(C)** $n = \left\{ \left(\frac{p}{x}\right)^{\left(\frac{1}{D}\right)} - 1 \right\} \times 100$

    **(D)** $n = \left\{ \left(\frac{p}{x}\right)^{\left(\frac{1}{D-1}\right)} - 1 \right\} \times 100$

    *Solve yourself:*

## Higher Order Thinking

**The following five questions are based on the following prompt.**

A boy throws a ball up from the top of a building. The height of the ball (in feet) above the ground $t$ seconds later is given by $h(t) = -t^2 + 2ta + b$.

91.  Which of the following denotes the time (in seconds) when the ball reaches the maximum height?

(A)  $a$

(B)  $b$

(C)  $a^2 - b$

(D)  $a^2 + b$

*Solve yourself:*

92.  Which of the following denotes the height of the building from which the ball was thrown?

(A)  $a$

(B)  $b$

(C)  $\dfrac{a}{b}$

(D)  $a^2 - b$

*Solve yourself:*

93.  What is the time (in seconds) when the ball, in its return path, is at a height equal to that of the building?

(A)  $a$

(B)  $\dfrac{b}{a}$

(C)  $2a$

(D)  $2a + b$

*Solve yourself:*

94.  In the return path of the ball, how long does the ball take to reach the ground level from when it was at a height equal to that of the building?

(A)   $2a - \sqrt{a^2 + b}$

(B)   $a - \sqrt{a^2 + b}$

(C)   $a + \sqrt{a^2 + b}$

(D)   $\sqrt{a^2 + b} - a$

*Solve yourself:*

95.  The ball reaches a maximum height of 25 feet after 4 seconds. After how much time (in seconds) will the ball reach the ground level?

(A)   1

(B)   4

(C)   9

(D)   16

*Solve yourself:*

**The following two questions are based on the following prompt.**

The graph shown below shows the number of bacteria ($y$), in thousands, in an experiment over a period of time ($x$) (in hours):

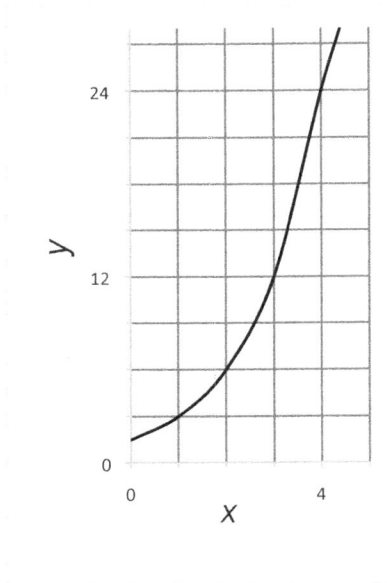

96. If the above graph represents $y = ab^x$, where $y$ is the number of bacteria in thousands and $x$ is the time in hours, what is the value of $(a + b)$?

    (A)   1.5

    (B)   2

    (C)   3.5

    (D)   4

    *Solve yourself:*

97. After minimum how many hours from the beginning of the experiment are the number of bacteria at least 10 times the number of bacteria present after 30 minutes from the start of the experiment?

    (A)   Between 1 and 2 hours

    (B)   Between 2 and 3 hours

    (C)   Between 3 and 4 hours

    (D)   Between 4 and 5 hours

*Solve yourself:*

**The following three questions are based on the following prompt.**

A sum of money, $P$, is invested in a bank under compound interest at $r\%$ rate of interest. The value, $V$, of the investment, $n$ years later is given by the formula: $V = P\left(1 + \dfrac{r}{100}\right)^{n}$.

**98.** Which of the following is the correct expression for the rate of interest, $r$, in terms of $V$, $P$ and $n$?

(A) $r = 100\left(\dfrac{P}{V}\right)^{\left(\frac{1}{n}\right)} - 100$

(B) $r = 100\left(\dfrac{V}{P}\right)^{n} - 100$

(C) $r = 100\left(\dfrac{V}{P}\right)^{\left(\frac{1}{n}\right)} - 1$

(D) $r = 100\left(\dfrac{V}{P}\right)^{\left(\frac{1}{n}\right)} - 100$

*Solve yourself:*

**99.** Which of the following gives the correct expression for the interest accumulated in the 2\textsuperscript{nd} year?

(A) $\dfrac{Pr^2}{100^2}$

(B) $\dfrac{Pr(100 + r)}{100^2}$

(C) $\dfrac{Pr(200 + r)}{100^2}$

(D) $\dfrac{Pr(100 + r)}{100}$

*Solve yourself:*

**100.**   For the same sum of money, in another bank, the rate of interest is $\left(\dfrac{r}{2}\right)$%. If the first bank takes
$n$ years to increase the sum of money by 33.1% and the other bank takes $m$ years to increase
the same sum of money by 33.1%, which of the following is true about $m$ and $n$?

   **(A)**   $n < m < 2n$

   **(B)**   $m = 2n$

   **(C)**   $m \geq 2n$

   **(D)**   $m > 2n$

   *Solve yourself:*

# Chapter 5

# Answer key

| (1) C | (26) 12 | (51) C | (76) C |
|-------|---------|--------|--------|
| (2) B | (27) D | (52) 6 | (77) A |
| (3) D | (28) C | (53) D | (78) B |
| (4) D | (29) A | (54) D | (79) C |
| (5) C | (30) C | (55) C | (80) D |
| (6) 27 | (31) D | (56) C | (81) D |
| (7) 14 | (32) A | (57) B | (82) D |
| (8) A | (33) B | (58) D | (83) B |
| (9) D | (34) 18 | (59) C | (84) B |
| (10) .833 | (35) B | (60) D | (85) D |
| (11) 4 | (36) D | (61) 1 | (86) C |
| (12) 9 | (37) D | (62) C | (87) C |
| (13) D | (38) B | (63) 10 | (88) C |
| (14) C | (39) C | (64) D | (89) D |
| (15) A | (40) 3 | (65) C | (90) D |
| (16) 4 | (41) C | (66) D | (91) A |
| (17) 10 | (42) 7 | (67) A | (92) B |
| (18) B | (43) D | (68) D | (93) C |
| (19) B | (44) D | (69) D | (94) D |
| (20) C | (45) D | (70) 6 | (95) C |
| (21) B | (46) 7 | (71) C | (96) C |
| (22) A | (47) B | (72) D | (97) C |
| (23) 20cm | (48) D | (73) B | (98) D |
| (24) C | (49) B | (74) A | (99) B |
| (25) C | (50) B | (75) C | (100) A |

# Chapter 6

# Solutions

1. We have:

$$p\left(1 + r^2\right)^3 = q$$

$$=> \left(1 + r^2\right)^3 = \frac{q}{p}$$

$$=> 1 + r^2 = \left(\frac{q}{p}\right)^{\frac{1}{3}}$$

$$=> r^2 = \left(\frac{q}{p}\right)^{\frac{1}{3}} - 1$$

$$=> r = \left\{\left(\frac{q}{p}\right)^{\frac{1}{3}} - 1\right\}^{\frac{1}{2}}$$ (Since $r$ is given to be a positive quantity, the negative square root of $r^2$ is rejected)

The correct answer is option C.

2. We have:

$$x^2 - 2x + y^2 + 4y = 4$$

$$=> (x^2 - 2x + 1) + (y^2 + 4y + 4) = 4 + 4 + 1$$

$$=> (x - 1)^2 + (y + 2)^2 = 3^2$$

Thus, the radius of the above circle is 3.

Thus, the radius of the new circle is $2 \times 3 = 6$.

Thus, the required equation of the circle with radius 6 and center at $(-2,\ 5)$ is:

$$(x - (-2))^2 + (y - 5)^2 = 6^2$$

$$=> (x + 2)^2 + (y - 5)^2 = 36$$

$$=> x^2 + 4x + 4 + y^2 - 10y + 25 = 36$$

$$=> x^2 + 4x + y^2 - 10y = 7$$

The correct answer is option B.

3. Number of units $= s$

Average cost per unit $= \$ \left(3 + 2.5s\right)$

Thus, total cost = $ $(s \times (3 + 2.5s)) = \$ (3s + 2.5s^2)$

Selling price per unit = $\$p$

Thus, total selling price = $ \$ (s \times p)$

Thus, for profit, we should have the selling price greater than the cost price:

$s \times p > 3s + 2.5s^2$

$=> 3s + 2.5s^2 - ps < 0$

The correct answer is option D.

4. Savings in the first month = $\$x$

Since in each month he increases his savings by $\$y$, the total increase in the $10^{\text{th}}$ month, i.e. after 9 months of increasing savings = $ \$ (9y)$

Thus:

$z = x + 9y$

$=> y = \dfrac{z - x}{9}$

The correct answer is option D.

5. Initial number of bacteria = $n$

The number of bacteria doubles in every 20 minutes, i.e. $\frac{1}{3}$ of an hour.

Thus, the number of times the bacteria doubles in a period of $t$ hours = $\dfrac{t}{\left(\frac{1}{3}\right)} = 3t$

Thus, the final number of bacteria

$= n \times 2^{3t}$

$=> m = n \times 2^{3t}$

$=> n = m \times 2^{-3t}$

The correct answer is option C.

6. Distance covered by the rocket in $t$ seconds = $3t^2$ miles.

Distance covered in the $5^{\text{th}}$ second

= (Distance covered in 5 seconds) − (Distance covered in 4 seconds)

Distance covered by the rocket in 5 seconds = $3 \times 5^2 = 75$ miles.

Distance covered by the rocket in 4 seconds = $3 \times 4^2 = 48$ miles.

Thus, (required distance) = $75 - 48 = 27$ miles.

The correct answer is 27.

7.  $x^2 - 2x - 15 = 0$

    $=> x^2 - 5x + 3x - 15 = 0$

    $=> x(x - 5) + 3(x - 5) = 0$

    $=> (x + 3)(x - 5) = 0$

    $=> x = -3$, or 5

    Now since it is given that the roots are $a$ and $b$, where $a > b$, we have:

    $a = 5, \ b = -3$

    $=> a + b^2 = 5 + 9 = 14$

    The correct answer is 14.

8.  $x^2 - (b + c)x + bc = 0$

    $=> x^2 - bx - cx + bc = 0$

    $=> x(x - b) - c(x - b) = 0$

    $=> (x - c)(x - b) = 0$

    $=> x = c$ or $b$

    Since the roots are equal in magnitude but opposite in sign, the sum of the roots must be '0'.

    $=> b + c = 0$

    $=> b = -c$

    The correct answer is option A.

9. $x^2 - 10x + 16 = 0$

   $=> x^2 - 2x - 8x + 16 = 0$

   $=> x(x - 2) - 8(x - 2) = 0$

   $=> (x - 2)(x - 8) = 0$

   $=> x = 2$ or $8$

   So, either $a = 2$ and $b = 8$ Or $a = 8$ and $b = 2$

   Note that in both cases, $(a + b)^2 = 10^2 = 100$

   And $(a - b)^2 = $ Either $(2 - 8)^2$ Or $(8 - 2)^2 = 36$

   Thus, the new roots are 100 and 36.

   Thus, the required equation:

   $=> x^2 - (100 + 36)x + 100 \times 36 = 0$

   $=> x^2 - 136x + 3600 = 0$

   The correct answer is option D.

10. $x^2 + 3x - 40 = 0$

    $=> x^2 + 8x - 5x - 40 = 0$

    $=> x(x + 8) - 5(x + 8) = 0$

    $=> (x - 5)(x + 8) = 0$

    $=> x = -8$ or $5 \ldots$ (i)

    $y^2 + 4y - 60 = 0$

    $=> y^2 + 10y - 6y - 60 = 0$

    $=> y(y + 10) - 6(y + 10) = 0$

    $=> (y - 6)(y + 10) = 0$

    $=> y = 6$ or $-10 \ldots$ (ii)

Thus, from (i) and (ii), to find the maximum value of $\frac{x}{y}$, the cases we should consider are:

1. $x = -8$ and $y = -10 \Rightarrow \dfrac{x}{y} = 0.8$

OR

2. $x = 5$ and $y = 6 \Rightarrow \dfrac{x}{y} = 0.833$

$\Rightarrow \dfrac{x}{y} = .833$

Comparing the two cases, we see that the maximum value of $\dfrac{x}{y}$ is .833.

The correct answer is .833.

11.  Let the roots be $m$ and $n$. Thus, we have:

$x^2 + px + 6 \equiv (x - m)(x - n)$

$\Rightarrow x^2 + px + 6 \equiv x^2 - (m + n)x + mn$

$\Rightarrow mn = 6$ and $p = -(m + n)$

Since the roots are integers, the only possible values of $m$ and $n$ are integer factor-pairs for 6:

- $mn = 6 = 1 \times 6 \Rightarrow p = -7$

- $mn = 6 = 2 \times 3 \Rightarrow p = -5$

- $mn = 6 = -1 \times -6 \Rightarrow p = 7$

- $mn = 6 = -2 \times -3 \Rightarrow p = 5$

Thus, there are 4 possible values of $p$.

The correct answer is 4.

12.  We know that in a quadratic equation $px^2 + qx + r = 0$, the sum of the roots is given by $\left(-\frac{q}{p}\right)$ and the product of the roots is given by $\left(\frac{r}{p}\right)$.

Thus, in the above equation, we have sum of the roots $= -\dfrac{(a + 1)}{1} = -5 \Rightarrow a = 4$

The product of the roots in the above equation is given by $\dfrac{a + 5}{1} = 4 + 5 = 9$.

The correct answer is 9.

13.   Let us assume $3^x = k$.

      Thus, $9^x = (3^x)^2 = k^2$ and $3^{x+1} = 3 \times 3^x$.

      Hence, our equation becomes:

      $k^2 - 3k - 54 = 0$

      $=> k^2 - 9k + 6k - 54 = 0$

      $=> k(k-9) + 6(k-9) = 0$

      $=> (k+6)(k-9) = 0$

      $=> k = -6 \text{ or } 9$

      Thus, we have: $3^x = -6 \text{ or } 3^x = 9$.

      Since $3^x$ is always positive, we can reject the possibility of $3^x = -6$ and conclude that $3^x = 9$.

      Thus, $9^x = 9^2 = 81$

      The correct answer is option D.

14.   We have $x^2 - 2x - 24 < 0$

      $=> x^2 - 6x + 4x - 24 < 0$

      $=> (x-6)(x+4) < 0$

      The product of two numbers is negative if one of the numbers is positive and the other is negative.

      This implies:

      Either:
      $(x-6) < 0$ and $(x+4) > 0$

      $=> x < 6$ and $x > -4$

      $=> -4 < x < 6 \dots \dots (i)$

      Or:
      $(x-6) > 0$ and $(x+4) < 0$

      $=> x > 6$ and $x < -4$

But such a case is not possible where $x > 6$ as well as $x < -4$.

Therefore, the only possible values of $x$ are: $-4 < x < 6$

The integer values of $x$ that satisfy the inequality $-4 < x < 6$ are:

$-3, -2, -1, 0, 1, 2, 3, 4, \text{\&} 5$

Thus, there are nine possible integer values.

The correct answer is option C.

**15.** We have $f(x) = x^2 - 6x + 12$

$= x^2 - 2(x)(3) + 12$

$= x^2 - 2(x)(3) + 3^2 + 3$

$= (x - 3)^2 + 3$

Since $(x - 3)^2$ is a perfect square, it is non-negative.

Hence, the least value of $f(x)$ occurs if the perfect square term becomes zero (if $x = 3$).

In that case, the value of $f(x)$ becomes 3.

Thus, the least value of $f(x)$ is 3.

Hence, option A is true.

Again, since $f(x) = (x - 3)^2 + 3$ and $(x - 3)^2$ is non-negative, we can conclude that the value of $f(x)$ for any value of $x$ will always be positive.

Hence, option B is false.

In a quadratic equation $ax^2 + bx + c = 0$, the roots are real if $b^2 - 4ac = 0$.

Here, $a = 1$, $b = -6$, $\text{\&}$ $c = 12$.

Thus: $b^2 - 4ac = 36 - 48 = -12 < 0$.

Thus, the roots of the equation $f(x) = 0$ i.e. $3x^2 - 6x + 8 = 0$ are imaginary.

Hence, option C is false.

The correct answer is option A.

**16.** We have:

$$h(t) = -t^2 + 8t + 10$$

$$= -(t^2 - 8t) + 10$$

$$= -(t^2 - 2 \times 4t) - 16 + 16 + 10$$

$$= -(t^2 - 2 \times 4 \times t + 4^2) + 26$$

$$= -(t - 4)^2 + 26$$

Since $(t - 4)^2$ is a perfect square, its value is either positive or zero.

Thus, $-(t - 4)^2$ is either negative or zero.

Hence, for $h(t)$ to have the maximum value, the value of $-(t - 4)^2$ should be zero.

Thus: $-(t - 4)^2 = 0$

$=> t = 4$ seconds

Thus, the ball would reach the maximum height above the ground level after 4 seconds.

The correct answer is 4.

**17.** As per the given problem, $h(t) = -t^2 + 4t + 6$

$$=> h(t) = -(t^2 - 4t) + 6$$
$$=> h(t) = -(t^2 - 2 \times 2t) - 4 + 4 + 6$$
$$=> h(t) = -(t^2 - 2 \times 2 \times t + 2^2) + 10$$
$$=> h(t) = -(t - 2)^2 + 10$$

Since $(t - 2)^2$ is a perfect square, its value is always non-negative.

Thus, $-(t - 2)^2$ is always non-positive.

Hence, for $h(t)$ to have the maximum value, the value of $-(t - 2)^2$ should be zero.

Thus: $-(t - 2)^2 = 0$

$=> t = 2$ seconds

Hence the maximum height attained $= -(2 - 2)^2 + 10 = 10$ feet.

Thus, the ball would reach the maximum height of 10 feet above the ground level.

The correct answer is 10.

**18.**    We have: $h(t) = -(t-p)^2 + q$

Since $(t-p)^2$ is a perfect square, its value is always non-negative.

Thus, $-(t-p)^2$ is always non-positive.

Hence, for $h(t)$ to have the maximum value, the value of $-(t-p)^2$ should be zero; in that case the maximum height would be $q$ feet.

Thus, in the case of maximum height: $-(t-p)^2 = 0 => t = p$ seconds

Now we know that the maximum height was reached after 3 seconds.

Thus: $p = 3$.

Also, it is given that the maximum height reached is 16 feet.

Thus:

$q = 16$

We need to find the value of $t$ for which $h(t) = 0$

$=> -(t-3)^2 + 16 = 0$

$=> (t-3)^2 = 16$

$=> t - 3 = \pm 4$

$=> t = 3 \pm 4$

$=> t = 7$ or $-1$

Since time cannot be negative, we have $t = 7$ seconds

Thus, the ball reaches the ground level after 7 seconds.

The correct answer is option B.

**19.**    We have:

$\sqrt{x+2} + \sqrt{x-1} = 3$

$=> \left(\sqrt{x+2} + \sqrt{x-1}\right)^2 = 3^2$

$$\Rightarrow (x + 2) + (x - 1) + 2 \left( \sqrt{x + 2} \right) \left( \sqrt{x - 1} \right) = 9$$

$$\Rightarrow 2x + 1 + 2 \left( \sqrt{x + 2} \right) \left( \sqrt{x - 1} \right) = 9$$

$$\Rightarrow 2 \sqrt{(x + 2)(x - 1)} = 8 - 2x$$

$$\Rightarrow \sqrt{(x + 2)(x - 1)} = 4 - x$$

Again, squaring both sides, we get:

$$(x + 2)(x - 1) = (4 - x)^2$$

$$\Rightarrow (x^2 - x + 2x - 2) = 16 + x^2 - 8x$$

$$\Rightarrow (x^2 + x - 2) = 16 + x^2 - 8x$$

$$\Rightarrow 9x = 18$$

$$\Rightarrow x = 2$$

$$\Rightarrow x^2 = 2^2 = 4$$

**Alternate approach:**

$$\sqrt{x + 2} + \sqrt{x - 1} = 3$$

$$\Rightarrow \sqrt{x + 2} = 3 - \sqrt{x - 1}$$

Squaring both sides:

$$\Rightarrow x + 2 = 9 + (x - 1) - 6 \sqrt{x - 1}$$

$$\Rightarrow 2 + 1 - 9 = -6 \sqrt{x - 1}$$

$$\Rightarrow -6 = -6 \sqrt{x - 1}$$

$$\Rightarrow 1 = \sqrt{x - 1}$$

Squaring both sides again:

$$1 = x - 1$$

$$\Rightarrow x = 2$$

$$\Rightarrow x^2 = 2^2 = 4$$

The correct answer is option B.

**20.** We know that the sum of the roots of the equation $ax^2 + bx + c = 0$ is given by $\left(-\frac{b}{a}\right)$ and the product of the roots by $\left(\frac{c}{a}\right)$.

It is given that the roots of $3x^2 + 4x + 1 = 0$ are $p$ and $q$.

Thus, we have:

$$p + q = -\frac{4}{3} \text{ and } pq = \frac{1}{3}$$

Thus, we have:

$$(3 - 2p)(2q - 3)$$

$$= 6q - 9 - 4pq + 6p$$

$$= 6(p + q) - 4pq - 9$$

$$= 6\left(-\frac{4}{3}\right) - 4\left(\frac{1}{3}\right) - 9$$

$$= -8 - \frac{4}{3} - 9$$

$$= -\frac{55}{3}$$

The correct answer is option C.

**21.** It is given that the equation $x^2 + 6x + 8 = 0$ has two roots $p$ and $q$.

Thus, we have:

$$p + q = -\frac{6}{1} = -6 \dots \text{ (i)}$$

$$pq = \frac{8}{1} = 8 \dots \text{ (ii)}$$

The roots of equation $ax^2 + bx + c = 0$ are $\frac{1}{p}$ and $\frac{1}{q}$.

Sum of the roots $= -\frac{b}{a} = \left(\frac{1}{p} + \frac{1}{q}\right) = \frac{p+q}{pq} = -\frac{6}{8} = -\frac{3}{4}$

Product of the roots $= \frac{c}{a} = \left(\frac{1}{p} \times \frac{1}{q}\right) = \frac{1}{pq} = \frac{1}{8}$

Thus, the equation is:

$$x^2 - \left(-\frac{3}{4}\right)x + \left(\frac{1}{8}\right) = 0$$

$$=> 8x^2 + 6x + 1 = 0$$

If we multiply both sides of the above equation with positive integers like 2 or 4 or 20 etc. the resulting equation will still have the same roots and will have $a$, $b$, & $c$ as integers. However, we want the least value of $c$ that satisfies all the conditions for this equation. This value is 1.

Note: We cannot multiply both sides of the above equation with negative integers (say, $-1$) because then $a$ will become negative. We are given that $a > 0$.

The correct answer is option B.

22. Let us solve the equations and find out the roots.

$x^2 - 5x + 6 = 0$

$=> x^2 - 3x - 2x + 6 = 0$

$=> x\,(x - 3) - 2\,(x - 3) = 0$

$=> (x - 2)\,(x - 3) = 0$

$=> x = 3$ or 2

$y^2 + 6y - 7 = 0$

$=> y^2 + 7y - y - 7 = 0$

$=> y\,(y + 7) - 1\,(y + 7) = 0$

$=> (y - 1)\,(y + 7) = 0$

$=> y = 1$ or $-7$

On comparing the roots, we see that $x > y$ for both values of $x$ and $y$.

The correct answer is option A.

23. Let us find out the length of the rectangle first from where we would be able to calculate the breadth, and consequently the perimeter, of the rectangle.

Let the length of the rectangle be $x$ cm
Therefore, the breadth of the rectangle is $(x - 6)$ cm

Area of a rectangle = (Length of the rectangle) $\times$ (Breadth of the rectangle)

$=> x\,(x - 6) = 16$

$=> x^2 - 6x = 16$

$$=> x^2 - 6x - 16 = 0$$

$$=> x^2 - 8x + 2x - 16 = 0$$

$$=> x(x-8) + 2(x-8) = 0$$

$$=> (x-8)(x+2) = 0$$

$$=> x = 8 \text{ or } -2$$

Since $x$ is the length of the rectangle, it cannot be negative.

Hence $x = 8$ cm.

Thus, the sides of the rectangle are $x = 8$ cm and $(x-6) = 2$ cm.

Thus, the perimeter of the rectangle $= 2(8+2) = 20$ cm

Hence, the correct answer is 20 cm.

24. At the points where $f(x)$ and $h(x)$ intersect, the values of the functions will be equal.

Thus the points where these two graphs meet will satisfy the condition $f(x) = h(x)$

$$=> x^2 + 6x + 8 = 32 + 4x$$

$$=> x^2 + 2x - 24 = 0$$

$$=> x^2 + 6x - 4x - 24 = 0$$

$$=> x(x+6) - 4(x+6) = 0$$

$$=> (x-4)(x+6) = 0$$

$$=> x = 4 \text{ or } -6$$

Thus, the two graphs intersect at two points, $x = 4$ and $x = -6$.

The correct answer is option C.

25. An extraneous solution is a solution that emerges from the process of solving the problem but is not a valid solution to the original problem.

We have:

$$x - 3 = \sqrt{x^2 - 3}$$

Squaring both sides:

$x^2 - 6x + 9 = x^2 - 3$

$=> 6x = 12$

$=> x = 2$

We observe that there is only one solution for $x$.

Substituting $x = 2$ in the given equation, we have:

Left Hand Side $= 2 - 3 = -1$

Right Hand Side $= \sqrt{x^2 - 3} = \sqrt{2^2 - 3} = \sqrt{4 - 3} = \sqrt{1} = 1$

(Note: By definition, the '$\sqrt{\phantom{x}}$' symbol returns only the positive square root).

Thus, for $x = 2$, LHS $\neq$ RHS.

Since there is no other solution, the above equation has no solutions at all.

Thus, the extraneous solution is $x = 2$.

The correct answer is option C.

26.  Let one of the numbers be $x$. Therefore, the next odd number will be two more than that, hence $(x + 2)$.

   As per the problem, therefore we have $x^2 + (x + 2)^2 = 74$

   $=> x^2 + x^2 + 4x + 4 = 74$

   $=> 2x^2 + 4x - 70 = 0$

   $=> x^2 + 2x - 35 = 0$

   $=> x^2 + 7x - 5x - 35 = 0$

   $=> x(x + 7) - 5(x + 7) = 0$

   $=> (x + 7)(x - 5) = 0$

   $=> x = -7 \text{ or } 5$

   Since it is given that the integers are positive, we have: $x = 5$

Hence, the two numbers are 5 and 7.

The sum of the digits therefore is 12.

Hence, the correct answer is 12.

**27.** Let the length of the field be $x$ m.

Therefore, from the given problem, we have the original width as $(x - 16)$ m.

Therefore, the area of the field is $x(x - 16)$ m$^2$.

In the figure here, the football field is represented by the inner rectangle. This rectangle is surrounded by a track 2-meter-wide on all sides.

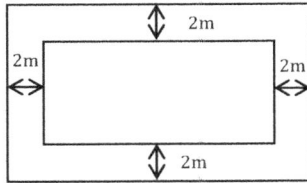

Thus, the length and width of the outer rectangle $= (x + 4)$ m and $(x - 16 + 4) = (x - 12)$ m.

Thus, the total area enclosed by the outer rectangle $= (x + 4)(x - 12)$ m$^2$

Thus, the area of the track

$$= (x + 4)(x - 12) - x(x - 16)$$

$$= (x^2 - 8x - 48 - x^2 + 16x)$$

$$= 8(x - 6)$$

Since this is $\frac{1}{3}$ of the football field's area, we have:

$$8(x - 6) = \frac{1}{3}x(x - 16)$$

$$\Rightarrow 24x - 144 = x^2 - 16x$$

$$\Rightarrow x^2 - 40x - 144 = 0$$

$$\Rightarrow (x - 36)(x - 4) = 0$$

$$\Rightarrow x = 4 \text{ or } 36$$

However, $x$ must be greater than 16 else the width would be negative.

Thus, we have: $x = 36$ m

Therefore, the length of the field = 36 m

The correct answer is option D.

28. Let the cost of each orange be $\$x$.

Therefore, the number of oranges bought by Peter = $\left(\frac{144}{x}\right)$.

If the cost of each orange would have been \$2 less, he would have got $\left(\frac{144}{x-2}\right)$

Thus we have:

$$\frac{144}{x-2} - \frac{144}{x} = 12$$

$$=> \frac{1}{x-2} - \frac{1}{x} = \frac{12}{144}$$

$$=> \frac{x-x+2}{x(x-2)} = \frac{1}{12}$$

$$=> x(x-2) = 24$$

$$=> x^2 - 2x - 24 = 0$$

$$=> x^2 - 6x + 4x - 24 = 0$$

$$=> x(x-6) + 4(x-6) = 0$$

$$=> (x+4)(x-6) = 0$$

$$=> x = -4 \text{ or } 6$$

Since $x$ is the price of an orange, it cannot be negative.

Thus, we have: $x = 6$

Thus the number of oranges bought by Peter is $\left(\frac{144}{6}\right) = 24$

The correct answer is option C.

29. It is given in the problem that there are two costs involved viz. Production cost and Warehousing cost.

Therefore, the total cost of producing $n$ number of speakers is $f(n) + g(n)$.

Therefore, the total cost = $ ($n^2 + 14n + n^2 + 2n$) = $($2n^2 + 16n$).

Selling price of $n$ products will be $ ($40n$).

Therefore, profit $P$ after selling $n$ products is $P = $ $\left[40n - (2n^2 + 16n)\right]$.

We need to find out $n$ at which the profit is maximum.

Thus, we have:

$P = 40n - (2n^2 + 16n)$

$= 40n - 2n^2 - 16n$

$= -2n^2 + 24n$

$= -2\left(n^2 - 12n\right)$

$= -2\left(n^2 - 2 \times 6 \times n + 6^2 - 6^2\right)$

$= -2(n - 6)^2 + 2 \times 6^2$

$= -2(n - 6)^2 + 72$

In order to maximize the profit, we should minimize the negative part of the expression i.e. $\left\{-2(n - 6)^2\right\}$ should be minimum, i.e. zero.

$=> 2(n - 6)^2 = 0$

$n = 6$

Thus the maximum profit is when 6 million articles are sold by the manufacturer.

The correct answer is option A.

30.   If the man drives at $x$ miles per hour, he takes $(x + 2)$ hours.

Therefore, the total distance travelled

$= x(x + 2)$ miles

Now it is given that if he increases his speed by $y$ miles per hour, he would take $2y$ hours less than before.

Thus, we have:

$$x(x+2) = (x+y)\left(x+2-\frac{3y}{4}\right)$$

$$=> x^2 + 2x = x^2 + 2x - \frac{3xy}{4} + xy + 2y - \frac{3y^2}{4}$$

$$=> \frac{3y^2}{4} - 2y = \frac{xy}{4}$$

$$=> y(3y-8) = xy$$

$=> 3y - 8 = x$ (Cancelling $y$ from both sides; we can do such cancelling since we are given that $y \neq 0$)

$$=> x = 3y - 8$$

The correct answer is option C.

**31.**  $ax^2 - 36 = 0$

$$=> x^2 = \frac{36}{a}$$

$$=> x = \pm\frac{6}{\sqrt{a}}$$

Since the roots are integers, $a$ must be a perfect square and $\sqrt{a}$ should be a factor of 6.

Case 1: $x = \frac{6}{\sqrt{a}}$

Here, the root will be an integer less than 2 only for $\sqrt{a} = 6$

Case 2: $x = -\frac{6}{\sqrt{a}}$

Here, the root will be an integer less than 2 for $\sqrt{a} = 1,\ 2,\ 3$ and 6.

Thus, combining the two cases,

Possible values of $\sqrt{a}$ are: 1, 2, 3 and 6 (Note: $\sqrt{*}$ by definition takes only positive values)

Squaring, we have:

Possible values of $a$ are: 1, 4, 9 and 36

The correct answer is option D.

**32.**  $\frac{1}{2}\left(\frac{1}{x-4}\right)(x^2 - 16) = \left(1 + \frac{4}{x-4}\right)(x-4)$

$$=> \frac{1}{2(x-4)}(x+4)(x-4) = \frac{(x-4+4)}{(x-4)}(x-4)$$

Since $(x-4)$ is in the denominator, we have: $x-4 \neq 0$

Thus, cancelling $(x-4)$ from both sides:

$$\frac{(x+4)}{2} = x$$

$$=> x = 4$$

However, $x \neq 4$ since in the original equation, $(x-4)$ is in the denominator, as discussed before.

Thus, no real value of $x$ satisfies the given equation.

The correct answer is option A.

33. We know that the deposit is $10

Since the interest is $r\%$ in 3 years, we have:

Amount after 3 years = $\$\left\{10\left(1+\frac{r}{100}\right)\right\}$

In $n$ years, number of 3-year periods = $\left(\frac{n}{3}\right)$

Thus, the amount after $t$ years = $\$\left\{10\left(1+\frac{r}{100}\right)^{\left(\frac{n}{3}\right)}\right\}$

Hence, the correct answer is option B.

34. Let time taken be $t$ hours.

Number of 9-hour periods in $t$ hours = $\frac{t}{9}$

Number of 3-hour periods in $t$ hours = $\frac{t}{3}$

Final number of bacteria of the 1$^{st}$ strain = $1024 \times 2^{\left(\frac{t}{9}\right)}$

Final number of bacteria of the 2$^{nd}$ strain = $64 \times 2^{\left(\frac{t}{3}\right)}$

Thus: $1024 \times 2^{\left(\frac{t}{9}\right)} = 64 \times 2^{\left(\frac{t}{3}\right)}$

$$=> 2^{\left(\frac{t}{9}+10\right)} = 2^{\left(6+\frac{t}{3}\right)}$$

$$=> \frac{t}{9} + 10 = 6 + \frac{t}{3}$$

$$=> \frac{2t}{9} = 4 => t = 18$$

The correct answer is 18.

**35.** Let the number be $x$

$=> |x^2 - x| = 12$

$=> x^2 - x = \pm 12$

$=> x^2 - x + 12 = 0$ OR $x^2 - x - 12 = 0$

The first one has no real solution since the discriminant is negative

(Note: In the equation $ax^2 + bx + c$, the discriminant is $(b^2 - 4ac)$)

The second equation: $x^2 - x - 12 = 0$

$=> (x - 4)(x + 3) = 0$

$=> x = 4$ or $-3$

Thus, there is only one positive number.

The correct answer is option B.

**36.** The equations $x^2 + ax + b = 0$ and $x^2 + px + q = 0$ have both roots common if they represent the same equation, i.e. $a = p$ and $b = q$

Thus, we have:

$-6a = -4 => a = \frac{2}{3}$

$12 = 9b => b = \frac{4}{3}$

$=> a + b = \frac{2}{3} + \frac{4}{3} = 2$

The correct answer is option D.

**37.** Since $a^b = 1$, possible cases are:

$a = 1 => x - 3 = 1 => x = 4$ ... (i)

$b = 0 => x - 6 = 0 => x = 6$ ... (ii)

$a = -1$ and $b$ is even $=> x - 3 = -1 => x = 2$ (Here, $x - 6 = -4$, which is even)

Thus, the possible values of $x$ are: 4, 6, and 2

Required sum = 12

The correct answer is option D.

**38.** Given $x$ is a positive integer less than 4, possible values of $x$ are: 1, 2 and 3.

Working with possible values of $x$:

$x = 1$: LHS (Left Hand Side) of the given equation = 0; RHS (Right Hand Side) = 2 => LHS < RHS

$x = 2$: LHS = 4; RHS = 4 => LHS = RHS – satisfies

$x = 3$: LHS = 10; RHS = 8 => LHS > RHS

Thus, there is one such value of $x$.

The correct answer is option B.

**39.** $4^{(x^2-2x)} = 8^2$

$=> 2^{2(x^2-2x)} = 2^6$

$=> 2x^2 - 4x = 6$

$=> x^2 - 2x - 3 = 0$

$=> (x - 3)(x + 1) = 0$

$=> x = 3$ or $-1$

Thus, there are two real values of $x$.

The correct answer is option C.

**40.** $x^3 - 3x^2 + 4x - 12 = 0$

$=> x^2(x - 3) + 4(x - 3) = 0$

$=> (x^2 + 4)(x - 3) = 0$

Since $x^2 + 4 \neq 0 => x - 3 = 0 => x = 3$ (the only real root)

The correct answer is 3.

**41.** The distance covered by the ball in the $t^{\text{th}}$ second

= (Distance covered in $t$ seconds) – (Distance covered in $(t - 1)$ seconds) = $9t^2 - 9(t - 1)^2$

= $9\left\{t^2 - (t - 1)^2\right\}$

$$= 9 \left( t - (t - 1) \right) \left( t + (t - 1) \right)$$

$$= 9 \left( 2t - 1 \right)$$

Thus, we have:

$$9 \left( 2t - 1 \right) = h$$

$$=> 2t - 1 = \frac{h}{9}$$

$$=> t = \tfrac{1}{2} \left( \tfrac{h}{9} + 1 \right)$$

The correct answer is option C.

**42.**   We know that $x = 3$ satisfies the equation $x^2 - px + 12 = 0$

Substituting $x = 3$ in the equation, we have:

$$(3)^2 - p\,(3) + 12 = 0$$

$$=> 3p = 21$$

$$=> p = 7$$

The correct answer is 7.

**43.**   To find the point of intersection, we need to solve the two equations:

$$=> x^2 + 3x + 1 = x + 1$$

$$=> x^2 + 2x = 0$$

$$=> x\,(x + 2) = 0$$

$$=> x = 0 \text{ or } -2$$

The corresponding $y$ values are obtained by substituting the $x$ values in $y = x + 1$ (or in the other equation):

$$x = 0 => y = 1$$

$$x = -2 => y = -1$$

So, the given curve and line intersect at these two points: $(0, 1)$ and $(-2, -1)$.

Thus, the point closer to the X-axis has $y = 1$.

The correct answer is option D.

**44.**   We know that $f(1) = 2$

$$=> (1)^2 + b(1) + c = 2$$

$$=> b + c = 1 \ldots \text{(i)}$$

We also know that $f(2) = 0$

$$=> 2^2 + 2b + c = 0$$

$$=> 2b + c = -4 \ldots \text{(ii)}$$

Thus, from (i) and (ii), we have:

$$b = -5$$

$$c = 6$$

$$=> f(x) = x^2 - 5x + 6$$

$$=> f(0) = 6$$

The correct answer is option D.

**45.**   We have: $f(-2) = f(2)$

$$=> -8 + 2k + 2 = 8 - 2k + 2$$

$$=> k = 4$$

The correct answer is option D.

**46.**   We need to find the values of $x$ so that the function $f(x)$ has a real value.

Since $f(x) = \sqrt{9 - x^2}$, the square root must have non-negative values inside the root.

Thus, we have: $9 - x^2 = 0 => x^2 = 9 => -3 = x = 3$

$=>$ The values of $x$ are: $-3, -2, -1, 0, 1, 2, \& 3$

Thus there are 7 possible integer values of $x$.

The correct answer is 7.

**47.** We know that $f(1) = 2$.

By substituting $x = 1$ in the four options, we observe that options A, B and D satisfy this condition:

Option A: $1^2 + 1 = 2$

Option B: $3(1) - 1 = 2$

Option C: $1 + 4 = 5 \neq 2$

Option D: $1^3 + 1 = 2$

Again, from the values in the table, we see that the $x$ values increase by 1 and the $f(x)$ values increase by 3 always.

This implies a linear relation.

The correct answer is option B.

**48.** We have:

$g(1) = 3$ and $f(1) = 5$

$f(g(1)) = f(3) = 3$

$g(f(1)) = g(5) = 7$

Thus, we have:

$f(g(1)) + g(f(1)) = 3 + 7 = 10$

The correct answer is option D.

**49.** We have:

$g(-2) + f(-2) = 2 \times (-2) = -4$

$\Rightarrow g(-2) = -4 - f(-2)$

Also, we have:

$f(-2) = |-2| + (-2) = 2 - 2 = 0$

$\Rightarrow g(-2) = -4 - 0 = -4$

The correct answer is option B.

**50.** Since $f(x)$ intersects the X-axis at $(1, 0)$ and $(5, 0)$, the roots of $f(x)$ are 1 and 5.

Thus, we have:

$f(x) = a(x - 1)(x - 5)$

Since $f(2) = 3$, we have:

$a(2 - 1)(2 - 5) = 3$

$=> a = -1$

$=> f(x) = -(x - 1)(x - 5)$

$=> f(4) = -(4 - 1)(4 - 5) = 3$

The correct answer is option B.

**Alternate approach:**

Like every quadratic function, the function $f(x)$ is symmetric about the line passing through the mid-point of the roots, i.e. $x = \frac{1+5}{2} = 3$

Since $x = 2$ and $x = 4$ are equidistant from $x = 3$, we have:

$f(4) = f(2) = 3$

**51.** We have:

$$f(x) = \frac{1}{\sqrt{1 - x^2} - 1}$$

For the above function to be defined, the term under the 'square root' must be non-negative.

Thus, we have:

$1 - x^2 \geq 0$

$=> x^2 \leq 1$

Thus, the possible values of $x$ are: $-1, 0, 1 \ldots$ (i)

However, we also need to ensure that the denominator of the expression for $f(x)$ is non-zero.

Thus, we have:

$\sqrt{1 - x^2} - 1 \neq 0$

$$=> \sqrt{1-x^2} \neq 1$$

$$=> 1 - x^2 \neq 1$$

$$=> x^2 \neq 0$$

$$=> x \neq 0 \dots \text{(ii)}$$

Thus, from (i) and (ii), we have:

The possible values of $x$ are: $-1$ & $1$

The correct answer is option C.

52.  We have: $f(x) = ax^2 + x$

Since $f(1) = f(0) + 2$, we have:

$$a(1^2) + 1 = a(0)^2 + (0) + 2$$

$$=> a + 1 = 2$$

$$=> a = 1$$

$$=> f(x) = x^2 + x$$

$$=> f(2) = 2^2 + 2 = 6$$

The correct answer is 6.

53.  We have: $x = \sqrt{3} - 1$

$$=> x + 1 = \sqrt{3}$$

Squaring both sides:

$$(x + 1)^2 = \left(\sqrt{3}\right)^2$$

$$=> x^2 + 2x + 1 = 3$$

$$=> x^2 + 2x = 2$$

The correct answer is option D.

54. We have:

$a^2 + b^2 + 4a + 2b = 0 \dots$ (i)

$|a - b| = 0$

$=> a - b = 0$

$=> a = b$

Substituting $a = b$ in (i):

$a^2 + a^2 - 4a - 2a = 0$

$=> 2\left(a^2 - 3a\right) = 0$

$=> a\left(a - 3\right) = 0$

$=> a = 3$ (This is the only possible value of $a$ that satisfies $a\left(a - 3\right) = 0$ because given: $a \neq 0$)

$=> a + b = 3 + 3 = 6$

The correct answer is option D.

55. We have: $x$, $y$ are positive integers such that $x + y = 4$

Thus, possible values of $x$ and $y$ are: $(1, 3)$, $(2, 2)$ and $(3, 1)$

Thus, we have:

$z = x^2 + y^2$

If $x = 1, y = 3$, then: $z = 1^2 + 3^2 = 10$

If $x = 2, y = 2$, then: $z = 2^2 + 2^2 = 8$

If $x = 3, y = 1$, then: $z = 3^2 + 1^2 = 10$

Thus, the minimum value of $z = 8$

The correct answer is option C.

**56.** We have:

$2x + y = 8$

$=> y = 8 - 2x$

Since $x$ and $y$ are positive integers, the possible $(x, y)$ values are:  $(3, 2)$, $(2, 4)$, $(1, 6)$

$z = x^2 - y^2$

Thus, $z$ will be maximum if $x > y$, i.e. for $x = 3, y = 2$

$=> \max z = 3^2 - 2^2 = 5$

The correct answer is option C.

**57.** We know that $f(1) = 1$.

$f(2) = (-1)^2 \times f(2-1) = (-1)^2 \times f(1) = 1 \times 1 = 1$

$f(3) = (-1)^3 \times f(3-1) = (-1)^3 \times f(2) = (-1) \times 1 = -1$

$f(4) = (-1)^4 \times f(4-1) = (-1)^4 \times f(3) = 1 \times (-1) = -1$

$f(5) = (-1)^5 \times f(5-1) = (-1)^5 \times f(4) = (-1) \times (-1) = 1$

$f(6) = (-1)^6 \times f(6-1) = (-1)^6 \times f(5) = 1 \times 1 = 1$

$f(7) = (-1)^7 \times f(7-1) = (-1)^7 \times f(6) = (-1) \times 1 = -1$

The correct answer is option B.

**58.**

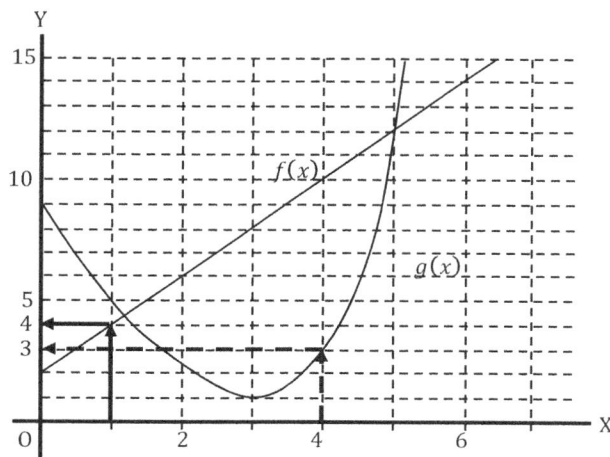

From the graph: $f(1) = 4$

Thus, we have: $k = 4$

$=> g(k) = g(4) = 3$ (from the graph)

The correct answer is option D.

59. We have:

$$\frac{1}{\sqrt{a+1} + \sqrt{a}}$$

$$= \frac{(\sqrt{a+1} - \sqrt{a})}{(\sqrt{a+1} + \sqrt{a})(\sqrt{a+1} - \sqrt{a})}$$

$$= \frac{\sqrt{a+1} - \sqrt{a}}{(\sqrt{a+1})^2 - (\sqrt{a})^2}$$

$$= \frac{\sqrt{a+1} - \sqrt{a}}{(a+1) - (a)}$$

$$= \sqrt{a+1} - \sqrt{a}$$

The correct answer is option C.

60. Working with the options, we have:

- Option A: $f(x) = x + 2$
  $=> f(a+1) = (a+1) + 2 = a + 3$
  $f(a) \times f(1) = (a+2)(1+2) = 3a + 6$
  Only for one specific value of $a$ will $a + 3$ be equal to $3a + 6$.
  Thus, $f(a+1) \neq f(a) \times f(1)$ for all values of $a$ – Option Rejected

- Option B: $f(x) = x^2$
  $=> f(a+1) = (a+1)^2$
  $f(a) \times f(1) = a^2 \times 1^2 = a^2$
  Thus, $f(a+1) \neq f(a) \times f(1)$ for all values of $a$ – Option Rejected

- Option C: $f(x) = 2x$
  $=> f(a+1) = 2(a+1) = 2a + 2$
  $f(a) \times f(1) = 2a \times 2 = 4a$
  Thus, $f(a+1) \neq f(a) \times f(1)$ for all values of $a$ – Option Rejected

- Option D: $f(x) = 2^x$
  $=> f(a+1) = 2^{(a+1)} = (2^a)(2^1) = f(a) \times f(1)$ – Satisfies for all values of $a$.

The correct answer is option D.

**61.** $f(g(x)) = \frac{g(x) - k}{5} = \frac{(5x+1) - k}{5} = \frac{5x + 1 - k}{5}$

Since $f(g(x)) = x$

$=> \frac{5x+1-k}{5} = x => 5x + 1 - k = 5x$

$=> k = 1$

The correct answer is 1.

**62.** We are given that $k$ is a constant. This means, the value of $k$ will be the same for all values of $x$. So, we can solve the question by taking some easy value of $x$, say $x = 0$.

Taking $x = 0$, we have:

$f(0) = -\frac{1}{k}$

Since given: $f(f(0)) = 0$, we have:

$$\frac{\left(-\frac{1}{k}\right) - 1}{2\left(-\frac{1}{k}\right) + k} = 0$$

$=> -\frac{1}{k} - 1 = 0$

$=> k = -1$

The correct answer is option C.

**63.** Given:

If $x$ is prime, $f(x) = f(x - 1) + 2$ .... 1st relation

If $x$ is non-prime, $f(x) = f(x - 1) + 1$ .... 2nd relation

For $x = 2$ (prime) : $f(2) = f(2 - 1) + 2 = f(1) + 2 = 5$ from the 1st relation

For $x = 3$ (prime) : $f(3) = f(3 - 1) + 2 = f(2) + 2 = 7$ from the 1st relation

For $x = 4$ (non $-$ prime) : $f(4) = f(4 - 1) + 1 = f(3) + 1 = 8$ from the 1st relation

For $x = 5$ (prime) : $f(5) = f(5 - 1) + 2 = f(4) + 2 = 10$ from the 2nd relation

The correct answer is 10.

**64.** $f(x) = \frac{2^x + 1}{2^x}$

$=> f(1) = \frac{2^1 + 1}{2^1} = \frac{2+1}{2} = \frac{3}{2}$

Also, $f(-1) = \frac{2^{-1} + 1}{2^{-1}} = 3$

The correct answer is option D.

**65.** $f(x + 1) = f(x) + x + \frac{1}{2}$

Substituting $x = 0$: $f(0 + 1) = f(0) + 0 + \frac{1}{2}$

$=> f(1) = f(0) + 1$

$=> a + b = b + \frac{1}{2}$

$=> a = \frac{1}{2}$

The correct answer is option C.

**Alternate approach:**

$f(x + 1) = f(x) + x + \frac{1}{2}$

$=> a(x + 1)^2 + b = (ax^2 + b) + x + \frac{1}{2}$

$=> a(1 + 2x) = x + \frac{1}{2}$

$=> a = \frac{x + \frac{1}{2}}{1 + 2x}$

$=> a = \frac{\frac{1}{2}(2x + 1)}{2x + 1}$

$=> a = \frac{1}{2}$

**66.** $\dfrac{f(1) \times f(2)}{f(3)}$

$= \dfrac{\left(2^{1-1} \times 2^{2-1}\right)}{2^{3-1}}$

$= \dfrac{2^0 \times 2^1}{2^2}$

$= 2^{-1} = 0.5$

The correct answer is option D.

**67.** Working with the statements:

 **I.** $f(0) = 0 - 0 = 0 => $ The graph passes through $(0, 0)$ i.e. the origin.

 **II.** Let us check the value of $f(x)$ for some $x$ values: $f(-1) = (-1)^5 - (-1)^2 = -1 - 1 = -2$
 Thus, the graph doesn't always lie above the X-axis.

 **III.** The graph would be symmetric if for every value of $x$, the value of $f(x)$ would be the same as that for $(-x)$, i.e. $f(x) = f(-x)$
 However, $f(-x) = (-x)^5 - (-x)^2 = -x^5 - x^2 \neq f(x)$
 Thus, the graph is not symmetric about the Y-axis.

The correct answer is option A.

**68.** The total cost of producing $n$ articles
$= f(n) + g(n) = \$ (-n^2 + 120n - n^2 + 60n) = \$(180n - 2n^2)$

Selling price of $n$ articles $= \$50n$

Therefore, profit after selling $n$ articles $= \$ [50n - (180n - 2n^2)] = \$ (2n^2 - 130n)$

The manufacturer will be said to have made a profit if the above expression for profit has a positive value. So, we have:

$2n^2 - 130n > 0$

$=> 2n(n - 65) > 0$

Since $n > 0$ (the manufacturer is *producing* articles; so $n$ is not zero. And, the number of articles cannot be negative.), we can divide both sides of the above inequality with $n$ without changing the sign of inequality:

$n - 65 > 0$

$=> n > 65$

The correct answer is option D.

**69.** We have: $x - 3 = \sqrt{x^2 - 15}$

Squaring both sides: $x^2 - 6x + 9 = x^2 - 15$

$=> 6x = 24$

$=> x = 4$

Substituting $x = 4$ in the given equation, we have:

Left Hand Side (LHS) = $4 - 3 = 1$

Right Hand Side (RHS) = $\sqrt{x^2 - 15} = \sqrt{4^2 - 15} = \sqrt{16 - 15} = 1$.

Thus, for $x = 4$, LHS = RHS. Thus, there is no extraneous solution.

The correct answer is option D.

**70.** Let one of the numbers be $x$.

Thus, the next odd number $= (x + 2)$.

Thus, we have:

$x^2 + (x + 2)^2 = 290$

$x^2 + x^2 + 4x + 4 = 290$

$2x^2 + 4x - 286 = 0$

$x^2 + 2x - 143 = 0$

$x^2 + 13x - 11x - 143 = 0$

$x\,(x + 13) - 11\,(x + 13) = 0$

$(x - 11)\,(x + 13) = 0$

$x = 11$ or $-13$

Since the integers are positive, $x = 11$.

Thus, the two numbers are 11 and 13, having sums of digits $(1 + 1) = 2$ and $(1 + 3) = 4$, respectively.

The number obtained by adding these two sums of digits therefore is $2 + 4 = 6$.

The correct answer is 6.

**71.** $(0.25)^x > (0.125)^{2x-3}$

$\Rightarrow \left(\frac{1}{4}\right)^x > \left(\frac{1}{8}\right)^{2x-3}$

$\Rightarrow \dfrac{1}{4^x} > \dfrac{1}{8^{(2x-3)}}$

$\Rightarrow 8^{(2x-3)} > 4^x$

$$=> 2^{3(2x-3)} > 2^{2x}$$

$$=> 6x - 9 > 2x$$

$$=> x > \frac{9}{4}$$

Thus, the least integer value of $x = 3$

The correct answer is option C.

72.  $x < y < -x$

$$=> x < -x$$

$$=> 2x < 0$$

$$=> x < 0$$

However, $y$ may be positive or negative.

Since $y^2 > 0$, we must have $xy^2 < 0$.

The correct answer is option D.

73.  $y = x^2 - x + 1$

$$= x^2 - 2x \left(\frac{1}{2}\right) + \left(\frac{1}{2}\right)^2 + \frac{3}{4}$$

$$= \left(x - \frac{1}{2}\right)^2 + \frac{3}{4}$$

Since $\left(x - \frac{1}{2}\right)^2 = 0$ (the square of any real number is non-negative), we have:

$$=> y > 0$$

Note: Options C and D can be invalidated by taking a simple example:

When $x = 1 : y = 1 - 1 + 1 = 1$

Thus, $x$ and $y$ can have the same values.

The correct answer is option B.

74.  $-\frac{19}{5} = 3a - 1 = \frac{17}{3}$

$$=> -\frac{19}{5} + 1 = 3a = \frac{17}{3} + 1$$

$$=> -\frac{14}{5} = 3a = \frac{20}{3}$$

$$=> -\frac{14}{15} = a = \frac{20}{9}$$

$$=> -\frac{14}{15} + 1 = a + 1 = \frac{20}{9} + 1$$

$$=> \frac{1}{15} = a + 1 = \frac{29}{9}$$

The integer values that satisfy this inequality are: $1, 2,$ & $3$.

Thus, in total, three integer values of $(a + 1)$ are possible.

The correct answer is option A.

**75.** $|x - 3| = 7$

$$=> -7 = x - 3 = 7$$

$$=> 3 - 7 = x = 7 + 3$$

$$=> -4 = x = 10$$

$$=> -4 - 1 = x - 1 = 10 - 1$$

$$=> -5 = x - 1 = 9$$

Therefore, the possible integer values that $x - 1$ can take are:
$\{-5, -4, -3, -2, -1, 0, 1, 2, ..., 7, 8, 9\}$

The corresponding values of $|x - 1|$ will be: $\{5, 4, 3, 2, 1, 0, 1, 2, ..., 7, 8, 9\}$

Thus, the possible integer values of $|x - 1|$ are $0, 1, 2, 3, 4, 5, 6, 7, 8$ and $9$.

A total of ten integer values are possible.

The correct answer is option C.

**76.** Amount after 3 years $= \$ \left\{ 1000 \left( 1 + \frac{r}{100} \right)^3 \right\}$

$$=> P = 1000 \left( 1 + \frac{r}{100} \right)^3$$

$$=> \left( 1 + \frac{r}{100} \right)^3 = \frac{P}{1000}$$

Taking cube root:

$$1 + \frac{r}{100} = \left(\frac{P}{1000}\right)^{\left(\frac{1}{3}\right)}$$

$$=> \frac{r}{100} = \left(\frac{P}{1000}\right)^{\left(\frac{1}{3}\right)} - 1$$

$$=> r = 100 \left\{ \left(\frac{P}{1000}\right)^{\left(\frac{1}{3}\right)} - 1 \right\}$$

The correct answer is option C.

77.  We have: $(0.25)^x < 2^{2-3x}$

$$=> \left(\frac{1}{4}\right)^x < 2^{(2-3x)}$$

$$=> 2^{2(-x)} < 2^{2-3x}$$

$$=> -2x < 2 - 3x$$

$$=> x < 2$$

Thus, the possible integer values of $x$ that fulfill this condition are: $\{1, 0, -1, -2, -3, -4\ldots\}$.

The second condition is that $|x| < 3$
$$=> -3 < x < 3$$

The possible integer values of $x$ that fulfill both conditions are: $1, 0, -1$, and $-2$.

$$=> \text{Required sum} = 1 + 0 + (-1) + (-2) = -2$$

The correct answer is option A.

78.

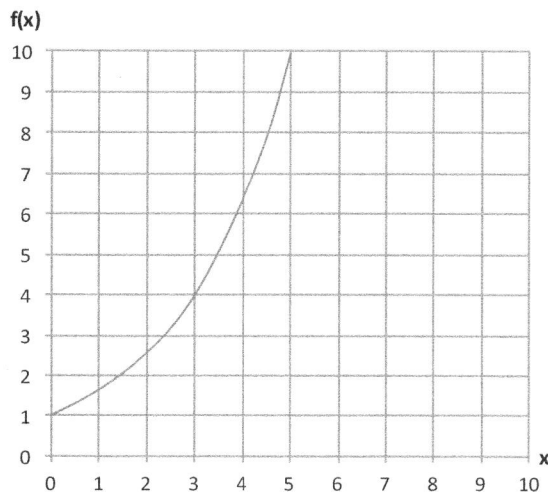

Assuming $y = 2^x$, we would have:

$x = 0$, $y = 1$; $x = 1$, $y = 2$; $x = 2$, $y = 4$; $x = 3$, $y = 8$, etc.

However, the values of $y$ for the above values of $x$ are less than (or equal to) the corresponding values of $y$ obtained above.

Thus, $p < 2$

If $0 < p < 1$, i.e. a fraction, the corresponding values of $y$ for higher values of $x$ would become smaller. Thus, the graph should not be an increasing one, but a decreasing one.

The correct answer is option B.

**Alternate approach:**

We have: $f(x) = p^x$

$=> f(1) = p$

From the graph, we see that $f(1)$ lies between 1 and 2

$=> 1 < p < 2$

79.  Distance travelled $= d$ miles.

Speed $= s$ miles per hour.

Thus, time taken $= \dfrac{d}{s}$ hours.

New speed $= (s + 10)$ miles per hour.

Thus, new time taken $= \dfrac{d}{(s+10)}$ hours.

Since he would have reached more than 1 hour earlier, we have:

$\frac{d}{s} - \frac{d}{s+10} > 1$

$=> d\left(\frac{1}{s} - \frac{1}{s+10}\right) > 1$

$=> \frac{d(s+10-s)}{s(s+10)} > 1$

$=> 10d > s(s + 10)$

$=> \frac{1}{10}s(s + 10) < d$

The correct answer is option C.

**80.** Distance on 1st day = $d$ units

Distance on 2nd day = $d \times \left(\frac{120}{100}\right) = d \times \left(\frac{6}{5}\right)$ units

Distance on 3rd day = $d \times \left(\frac{6}{5}\right)^2$ units; and so on

Thus, distance on the $n^{th}$ day = $d \times \left(\frac{6}{5}\right)^{n-1}$

We have: $d \times \left(\frac{6}{5}\right)^{n-1} > D$

$=> \left(\frac{6}{5}\right)^{n-1} > \frac{D}{d}$

$=> \left(\frac{D}{d}\right)^{\left(\frac{1}{n-1}\right)} < \frac{6}{5}$

The correct answer is option D.

**81.** We divide the number line in the four parts as shown:

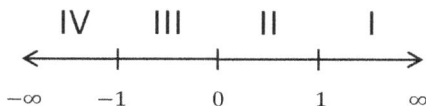

We now pick one number from each region (I, II, III and IV); if a number satisfies the given condition, the entire region corresponding to it will also satisfy.

Region I: Taking $x = 2$, the given inequality becomes: $4 > 128 > 2$ => Doesn't satisfy the given condition

Region II: Taking $x = \frac{1}{2}$: $\frac{1}{4} > \frac{1}{128} > \frac{1}{2}$ => Doesn't satisfy the given condition

Region III: Taking $x = -\frac{1}{2}$: $\frac{1}{4} > -\frac{1}{128} > -\frac{1}{2}$ => Satisfies the given condition

Region IV: Taking $x = -2$: $4 > -128 > -2$ => Doesn't satisfy the given condition

Thus, the correct region is: $-1 < x < 0$

Since $x$ is negative, statement I must be true since $x^2$ is positive while $x^3$ is negative.

The correct answer is option D.

**82.** We know that an even exponent of any number is always positive irrespective of whether the base number is positive or negative.

$a^5 b^4 c^3 d^6 = a^4 b^4 c^2 d^6 \times ac$, where $a^4 b^4 c^2 d^6$ is always positive => $ac < 0$

=> $a > 0$ and $c < 0$

OR

$a < 0$ and $c > 0$

That is, $a$ and $c$ have opposite positive/negative nature.

Working with options:

(A)  has the term: $ab$ => Can be rejected because the question gives no information about the positive/negative nature of $a$ and $b$

(B)  has the term: $b^2d$ => Can be rejected because the question gives no information about the positive/negative nature of $d$

(C)  has the term: $b^3c^2$ => Can be rejected because the question gives no information about the positive/negative nature of $b$

(D)  has the term: $a^3c^3 = a^2c^2 \times ac$ => Now $a^2c^2 > 0$ always and as, deduced above, $ac < 0$ => the product of $a^2c^2$ and $ac$ will indeed be negative: $a^3c^3 < 0$. Therefore, this option holds.

The correct answer is option D.

83.  From the number line, we can see that $p$ is negative; $q$ is positive; $r$ is positive; $s$ is positive.

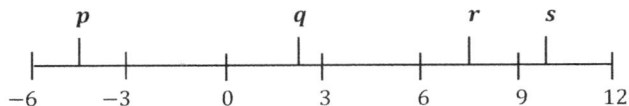

Working with options:

(A)  $ps$ is negative ($p$ is negative and $s$ is positive), while $q^2$ is positive – Incorrect

(B)  $qr$ is positive (both $q$ and $r$ are positive).
     (Maximum value of $qr$) < ($3 \times 9 = 27$)
     (Minimum value of $s^2$) > ($9^2 = 81$)
     => $qr < s^2$ – Correct

(C)  $pr$ is negative, while $s^2$ is positive – Incorrect

(D)  $rs$ is positive, while $p^3$ is negative – Incorrect

The correct answer is option B.

84. From the given equations, we need to remove the variable $y$. Thus, we multiply the first equation by $p$ and second equation by $q$.

Thus we get the following equations:

$$mp = p^2x - pqy$$

$$nq = q^2x - pqy$$

Subtracting the above two equations, we get

$$p^2x - q^2x = mp - nq$$

$$x = \frac{mp - nq}{p^2 - q^2}$$

The correct answer is option B.

85. We have:

$$-4 = x = 8 \dots \text{(i)}$$

$$-8 = y = 16 \dots \text{(ii)}$$

The minimum value of $\left(\frac{x}{y}\right)$ would be a negative number with the largest magnitude.

Thus, we take $x = 8$ and $y = -1 => \frac{x}{y} = -8$

The maximum value of $\left(\frac{x}{y}\right)$ would be a positive number with the largest magnitude.

Thus, we take $x = 8$ and $y = 1 => \frac{x}{y} = 8$

Thus, we have the required difference $= 8 - (-8) = 16$

The correct answer is option D.

86. We have:

$$x > 4 \text{ and } y > 8$$

$$=> x + y > 12$$

Thus, the least integer value is 13.

Possible values: $x = 4.5$, $y = 8.5$; or $x = 4.8$, $y = 8.2$; etc.

(Note: $x$ and $y$ are not necessarily integers)

The correct answer is option C.

87.   From the given equation, let us express $C$ in terms of $A$, $B$ and $D$:

We have:

$A \times \sqrt[3]{C} = \frac{B \times \sqrt{D}}{5}$

$=> \sqrt[3]{C} = \frac{B\sqrt{D}}{5A}$

$=> C = \left[\frac{B\sqrt{D}}{5A}\right]^3$

$=> C = \left[\frac{2 \times \sqrt{16}}{5 \times 5}\right]^3$

$=> C = \left(\frac{8}{25}\right)^3$

$=> C = \frac{512}{15625}$

The correct answer is option C.

88.   We know that the mass of the substance becomes half its initial value in every 42 seconds i.e. after 42 seconds, the mass of the substance $X$ will become $\frac{1}{2} \times 28$.

After yet another 42 seconds, i.e. after a total of 84 seconds, the mass will become $\left(\frac{1}{2} \times \left(\frac{1}{2} \times 28\right)\right)$ which is $\left\{\left(\frac{1}{2}\right)^2 \times 28\right\}$. The power on $\left(\frac{1}{2}\right)$ is equal to $\left(\frac{84}{42}\right) = 2$.

Number of '42 second' slots in 201 seconds $= \frac{210}{42} = 5$.

Thus, the final weight of the substance after 210 minutes

$= 28 \times \left\{\left(\frac{1}{2}\right) \times \left(\frac{1}{2}\right) \times \left(\frac{1}{2}\right) \ldots\ldots\ldots \left(\frac{210}{42} \text{ times}\right)\right\}$

$= 28 \times \left(\frac{1}{2}\right)^{\frac{210}{42}}$

$= 28 \times \left(\frac{1}{2}\right)^5$

The correct answer is option C.

89.   We have:

$F = \frac{GMm}{D^2} \ldots (i)$

The new distance, as per the given problem, is $2D$, and one of the masses, say, $M$ becomes $2M$.

Therefore, the new force denoted by $F' = \frac{G(2M)m}{(2D)^2} = \frac{GMm}{2D^2} \ldots (ii)$

Therefore, from equations (i) and (ii), we can say

$$F' = \frac{1}{2}\left(\frac{GMm}{D^2}\right)$$

$$=> F' = \tfrac{1}{2}F$$

Thus, the force becomes half of the initial value.

The correct answer is option D.

**90.** Number of pages the man typed on the first day = $x$.

Percent increase in the number of pages typed each day = $n\%$

Thus, number of pages typed on the second day = $x\left(1 + \dfrac{n}{100}\right)$

Since the man typed for $D$ days, this increase would happen for $(D-1)$ days after the first day.

Thus, the number of he typed on the last day = $x\left(1 + \dfrac{n}{100}\right)^{(D-1)}$

Thus, we have:

$$p = x\left(1 + \tfrac{n}{100}\right)^{D-1}$$

$$=> \left(1 + \tfrac{n}{100}\right)^{(D-1)} = \frac{p}{x}$$

$$=> 1 + \tfrac{n}{100} = \left(\frac{p}{x}\right)^{\left(\frac{1}{D-1}\right)}$$

$$=> n = \left\{\left(\frac{p}{x}\right)^{\left(\frac{1}{D-1}\right)} - 1\right\} \times 100$$

The correct answer is option D.

## Higher Order Thinking

91.  We have: $h(t) = -t^2 + 2ta + b$

$$=> h(t) = -(t^2 - 2ta + a^2) + a^2 + b$$

$$=> h(t) = -(t - a)^2 + (a^2 + b)$$

Since the square term '$(t - a)^2$' is negative, the maximum value of $h(t)$, i.e. the maximum height of the ball will be reached when the square term becomes '0'

$$=> t - a = 0$$

$$=> t = a$$

Note: The corresponding value of the maximum height is $(a^2 + b)$.

The correct answer is option A.

92.  We have: $h(t) = -t^2 + 2ta + b$

Thus, the height of the building is obtained by the height of the ball at $t = 0$

$$=> h(0) = b$$

The correct answer is option B.

93.  We know that the height of the building is $b$.

Thus, equating the height of the ball, at time $t$, to $b$, we have:

$$-t^2 + 2ta + b = b$$

$$=> -t(t - 2a) = 0$$

$$=> t = 0 \text{ or } t = 2a$$

$t = 0$ refers to the time when the ball was just thrown up. Thus, the other value of $t$ is the time when the ball was at the same height as that of the building.

The correct answer is option C.

94.  We have: $h(t) = -t^2 + 2ta + b$

From the previous question, we know that in the return path, the ball will be at a height equal to that of the building at $t = 2a \dots$ (i)

Also, when the ball is at ground level, we have:

$h(t) = 0$

$=> -t^2 + 2ta + b = 0$

$=> -(t-a)^2 + a^2 + b = 0$

$=> (t-a)^2 = a^2 + b$

$=> t - a = \pm\sqrt{a^2 + b}$

$=> t = a \pm \sqrt{a^2 + b}$

Since $t$ must be positive, we have: $t = a + \sqrt{a^2 + b}$ ... (ii)

Thus, the time required is the difference between the time when the ball is at ground level and when the ball is at a height equal to that of the building

$= \left(a + \sqrt{a^2 + b}\right) - 2a$

$= \sqrt{a^2 + b} - a$

The correct answer is option D.

**95.** From the first question, we know that:

Maximum height attained by the ball $= a^2 + b = 25$ ... (i)

Also, the maximum height is attained at $t = a = 4$ ... (ii)

Thus, from (i) and (ii):

$b = 25 - a^2 = 9$

$=> h(t) = -t^2 + 2at + b$

$=> h(t) = -t^2 + 8t + 9$

When the ball reaches the ground level, we have $h(t) = 0$

$=> 0 = -t^2 + 8t + 9$

$=> t^2 - 8t - 9 = 0$

$=> (t-9)(t+1) = 0$

$=> t = 9$ or $-1$

Obviously, the negative value of $t$ is unacceptable.

The correct answer is option C.

**96.** We have: $y = ab^x$

Observing values, we have: $x = 1 => y = 3$

$=> 3 = ab \dots$ (i)

Again, we have: $x = 2 => y = 6$

$=> 6 = ab^2 \dots$ (ii)

Dividing (ii) by (i):

$b = 2$

Thus, from (i):

$a = \dfrac{3}{2}$

Note: Thus, we have: $y = \dfrac{3}{2} \times 2^x$

Thus: $a + b = \dfrac{3}{2} + 2 = 3.5$

The correct answer is option C.

**97.** We know that:

$y = \dfrac{3}{2} \times 2^x$

The number of bacteria present 30 minutes after the start, i.e. $x = \dfrac{1}{2}$ is:

$y = \dfrac{3}{2} \times 2^{\left(\frac{1}{2}\right)}$

Since we need at least 10 times the above value, we have:

$\dfrac{3}{2} \times 2^x \geq 10 \times \dfrac{3}{2} \times 2^{\left(\frac{1}{2}\right)}$

$=> 2^x \geq 10 \times 2^{\left(\frac{1}{2}\right)}$

$=> 2^x \geq 10 \times 1.414$

$=> 2^x \geq 14.14$

At $t = 3$, we have: $2^x = 8$, which doesn't satisfy

At $t = 4$, we have: $2^x = 16 > 14.14$

Thus, the value of $t$ is between 3 hours and 4 hours.

The correct answer is option C.

98.  We have:

$$V = P\left(1 + \frac{r}{100}\right)^n$$

$$=> \left(1 + \frac{r}{100}\right)^n = \frac{V}{P}$$

Taking both sides to the power $\frac{1}{n}$, we have:

$$1 + \frac{r}{100} = \left(\frac{V}{P}\right)^{\left(\frac{1}{n}\right)}$$

$$=> \frac{r}{100} = \left(\frac{V}{P}\right)^{\left(\frac{1}{n}\right)} - 1$$

$$=> r = 100\left(\frac{V}{P}\right)^{\left(\frac{1}{n}\right)} - 100$$

The correct answer is option D.

99.  Amount after $n$ years:

$$V = P\left(1 + \frac{r}{100}\right)^n$$

Thus, the amount after 2 years

$$= P\left(1 + \frac{r}{100}\right)^2$$

Similarly, the amount after 1 year

$$= P\left(1 + \frac{r}{100}\right)^1$$

Thus, the interest accumulated in the 2nd year

= (Amount after 2 years) – (Amount after 1 year)

$$= P\left(1 + \frac{r}{100}\right)^2 - P\left(1 + \frac{r}{100}\right)^1$$

$$= P \left( 1 + \frac{r}{100} \right) \left\{ \left( 1 + \frac{r}{100} \right) - 1 \right\}$$

$$= P \left( 1 + \frac{r}{100} \right) \left( \frac{r}{100} \right)$$

$$= \frac{Pr\,(100 + r)}{100^2}$$

The correct answer is option B.

**100.**    Let us work with some values: $r = 10$

For the first bank, we have:

$$V = (1 + 33.1\%)\,P = 1.331P = P \left( 1 + \frac{10}{100} \right)^n$$

$$\Rightarrow (1.1)^n = 1.331$$

$$\Rightarrow n = 3$$

For the other bank, we have:

$$V = (1 + 33.1\%)\,P = 1.331P = P \left( 1 + \frac{(10/2)}{100} \right)^m$$

$$\Rightarrow (1.05)^m = 1.331$$

Working with values of $m$: $1.05^6 = 1.34$

Thus, the value of $m < 6$

$$\Rightarrow m < 2n$$

Obviously, $m$ must be greater than $n$

$$\Rightarrow n < m < 2n$$

The correct answer is option A.

# Chapter 7

# Talk to Us

## Have a Question?

Email your questions to info@manhattanreview.com. We will be happy to answer you. Your questions can be related to a concept, an application of a concept, an explanation of a question, a suggestion for an alternate approach, or anything else you wish to ask regarding the SAT.

Please do mention the page number when quoting from the book.

Best of luck!

Professor Dr. Joern Meissner
& The Manhattan Review Team

Made in the USA
Coppell, TX
21 December 2021

69548029R00070